GOD'S GRACE FOR
Daughters of Eve

To: April

Daughter of Eve ...
Child of God ...

By God's grace and for
His glory !

Sandie Abbott 2015

GOD'S GRACE FOR
Daughters of Eve

Lovers, Mothers and Others

Sandra A. Abbott

Grace Theology Press

God's Grace for Daughters of Eve

ISBN 10: 991658892
ISBN 13: 978-0-9916588-9-3
eISBN 10: 996561404
eISBN 13: 978-0-9965614-0-2

Special Sales: Most Grace Theology Press titles are available in special quantity discounts. Custom imprinting or excerpting can also be done to fit special needs. Contact Grace Theology Press at info@gracetheology.org.

Printed in the United States of America

*By God's grace and for His glory, this book is lovingly
dedicated to my husband Bill, to our son and daughter,
Kit and Jenni, and to all of our grandchildren.
Because of God's embrace of grace, we can be the face of grace,
and where we are can be the place of grace.*

DISCLAIMER

This book is based on events and characters from the Bible. While the appeal is universal, any resemblance to other actual persons, living or dead, is purely coincidental. The tone of this devotional book is of the author's own creation and is written to educate, entertain, and encourage.

ACKNOWLEDGEMENTS

A work like this would not have been possible without the teachings of my Phoenix Seminary professors including Dr. Fred Chay, Dr. Norm Wakefield, and Dr. T. Kem Oberholtzer. What you taught, and the way you taught, changed me forever.

My son Kit, a pastor and graduate of Western (now Phoenix) Seminary—earnestly encouraged me to take a course at seminary. This began a wonderful new season of my life.

Dr. Oberholtzer challenged me to actually take classes for credit and gave me the foundation for the rest of my education.Dr. Wakefield enriched my teaching, and some of his ideas inspired this book's Teaching Tips. While in Dr. Chay's classes, I learned to enjoy robust discussions on numerous biblical problem passages as we explored the many sides of contemporary theological issues. He would often say, "Count the days and make the days count, because right now counts forever." During my season of study at seminary, I was diagnosed and successfully treated for cancer. My focus on the Lord, in part through my seminary experience, sustained me.

Recently, through Grace Theology Press, Dr. Chay asked me to write a book. I am sincerely indebted to him, and to GTP, for giving me this opportunity to take what I learned, wrap it in a smile, and pass it on to others. With the excellent editing of Lucid Books, *God's Grace for Daughters of Eve* was born.

It is with profound gratitude to my family and friends that I acknowledge them, because they have made this book a reality by helping me proofread…one chapter at a time. My daughter Jenni has enthusiastically supported me in this adventure while we'd meet regularly for Bible study. For my Fellowship of Friends, your input has been greatly appreciated. All of you saw things I did not see.

Julie Abbott and I have been on parallel paths as we raced toward our goals while writing, re-writing, and writing again. Marianne Bayardi, thank you for the feedback you gave on the final lap of this race.

Above all, I thank my husband Bill, who faithfully supported me while I was having far more fun writing than either of us ever expected. For breakfasts and lunches while I communed with my computer and for daily walks long after dark, I offer my gratitude. Your wholehearted embrace of this new season of our lives has blessed me and our more than 50 years of marriage have amazed and awed me.

To all of you, I love you and thank you…Sandee

PREFACE

As God so often does, He takes the truth and wraps it around a person. This is theology in the form of biography. The most masterful expression of this is seen in the incarnation: Jesus becoming a man, that we might see and understand the grace of God.

Sandee Abbott creatively reveals through biblical biography the glorious grace of God manifested in both the Old and the New Testaments-for women. This provides the reader a platform from which to experience personally the grace of God, woven into the lives of His people, thus demonstrating His love and commitment to His children as He accomplishes His sovereign purposes.

As you read each chapter, a portrait of God's grace and God's power will emerge that will provide hope for you today, for it is the same all-powerful and all-loving Lord who invades our lives, and faithfully keeps His promises.

—Dr. Fred Chay, Grace School of Theology

CONTENTS

INTRODUCTION

Before the beginning, a plan began deep in the heart of God. He thought it and spoke it. He created something out of nothing that was everything. He made time, lived outside of time, but sometimes He entered into time, because after all…He had the time.

Then, at a point in time God walked and talked in a garden with the crown of His creation, made in His image; male and female, He had created them. They had been given everything they needed for life and liberty. They could have lived forever. Love ruled and grace reigned.

But there was a glitch. They had it all, except for just one little thing they could not have. It became the only thing they really wanted to have. When it was had, they hid. This was the end of the beginning. They did not get what they deserved, but they could not keep what they had.

Because the Creator of all knew all, in His omniscient love and great grace…He rescued His now perfectly imperfect children through a simple but earthshaking sacrifice. A Lamb was slain from the foundation of the world. This would suffice and satisfy the holiness of God, so that down through the corridors of time women and men could once again freely walk and talk with God who loves them. Grace abounds! Who could have loved them more?

In his *Chronicles of Narnia,* C. S. Lewis called humans the Daughters of Eve and the Sons of Adam. This devotional book is written through the perspective of God's grace for the Daughters of Eve. Grace is an unearned, unmerited, undeserved gift of God's unreasonable kindness. License ignores it, legalism wants to supervise it, but liberty requests it. God's grace is truly amazing.

Lessons linger and a line lasts which became a lifeline of love from the Father, to the Son, through the Spirit for all who would believe in the powerful promises of God—through grace alone, by faith alone, in Christ alone. It took a long time, but just at the right time that which was planned before time was braided into the tangles of time through the hand of God, by His grace and for His glory.

This is a story of Daughters of Eve: for men who marry them, sons who honor them, daughters who delight in them, people who pastor them, and above all...for women who are them.

God's Grace for the Girl in the Garden

She was there at the end of the beginning, and to be sure the guy in the Garden was the only man for Eve. "Wow!" may have been the first thing his soul said when first he saw her. Who could have loved her more?

God gave them everything except one thing, but with His gifts, He gave instructions. They were short: they were not to eat the fruit from the tree of the knowledge of good and evil. They simply were not allowed to do that one little thing. Somehow that perfect pair, those blessed ones, missed the mark the Maker made. They fell short. When offered that "one thing" by the evil one, Eve accepted and ate the first fruit of self-determination; Adam did as well.

The One who loved them more, cursed them not, but in compassion He gave consequences. Sin happened. Death in due season would come, but life lived on.

> *Here lies the tremendous mystery—that God should be all-powerful, yet refuse to coerce. He summons us to cooperation.*
>
> *—**Elisabeth Elliot**[1]*

1

They did not get what they deserved. Grace was given in the garden.

> **Genesis 3:14a and 15**
> So the Lord God said to the serpent: ... "I will put enmity between you and the woman, and between your seed and her Seed; He shall bruise your head, and you shall bruise His heel."

Then, their gloriously good God gave a prediction with a promise: even though the serpent would bruise a blessed baby of a Daughter of Eve, this offspring would crush the very head of the shimmering, seducing serpent. Concussions were real; this crushed cranium would be fatal and final one day, but not that day in the garden.

In other words, war was declared between the evil one and the woman. History proved correct: war walked down through the corridors of time, as evil challenged good. The Sons of Adam and the Daughters of Eve wandered through the valley of the shadow, yet the One who loved them more was with them. There was time for everything: a time to be born, and to die, to weep and to laugh, to mourn and to dance, to love and to hate.

As a Daughter of Eve, I like the laughing, loving, dancing times of life; I live for them and long for them, even in times of mourning, and weeping. Through it all, the One who loves me more is with me still, and stills my restless soul, by His grace and for His glory.

> **John 3:16-17**
> For God so loved the world that He gave His only begotten Son, that whoever believes in Him should not perish but have everlasting life. For God did not send His Son into the world to condemn the world, but that the world through Him might be saved.

This is possible because the God of unreasonable kindness and unending love made a prediction with a promise in the Garden of Eden. In another garden, the Garden of Gethsemane, both the prediction and the promise were on the line. The sacred Son of a Daughter of Eve, the Baby

2

of Bethlehem, the only Begotten of the Father, was the Man who never missed the mark.

He was perfect in every way. Jesus, the Lamb of God, slain before the foundation of the world, willingly walked the Via Delorosa to the cross. Death came since sin surfaced. But those who would believe in Him could truly live, because the sting of death died. Hope was resurrected on the third day and now life lives on, forever. Who could have loved us more?

That tremendous mystery, spoken of by Elisabeth Elliot, confounds us still: our all-powerful God refuses to coerce the Sons of Adam and the Daughters of Eve, yet He summons us to cooperation. Amazingly enough, when we do cooperate He rewards us lavishly, occasionally in this life, but far more likely in the life to come.

MEDITATION

Read several times, out loud, with a different vocal emphasis each time. Underline the emphasis you like best.

Genesis 1:27, 28a, and 31
So God created man in His own image; in the image of God He created him; male and female He created them. Then God blessed them....Then God saw everything that He had made, and indeed it was very good. So the evening and the morning were the sixth day.

Application

Put one line under the word **created**. Put two lines under the words **image of God**. Circle **very good**. What does that tell you about God? About grace? About you?

_____

How did God give grace to the Girl in the Garden?

_____

_____

Contemplation

Circle one question and explain: How do these verses comfort you? Correct you? Change you? Challenge you? Calm you?

_____

_____

Personal Prayer

Lord, thank You for creating me in Your image. Thank You for blessing me. Grant me the courage to cooperate with the good You have planned for me. Show Your grace to me today. Amen

TEACHING TIP

Look for the big picture in the lesson. When you teach, repeat that main idea throughout the lesson. For example, mention "grace abounds" (2-3 times) as you teach this chapter. The tighter the topic, the longer it might be remembered.

CHAPTER ONE NOTES

READ GENESIS CHAPTER ONE AND CHAPTER TWO.

Ecclesiastes 3:1, 4, and 8
To everything there is a season, a time for every purpose under heaven: A time to weep, and a time to laugh; a time to mourn, and a time to dance; A time to love, and a time to hate; time of war, and a time of peace.

Romans 5:6-18
For when we were still without strength, in due time Christ died for the ungodly. For scarcely for a righteous man will one die; yet perhaps for a good man someone would even dare to die. But God demonstrates His own love toward us, in that while we were still sinners, Christ died for us. Much more then, having now been justified by His blood, we shall be saved from wrath through Him.

For if when we were enemies we were reconciled to God through the death of His Son, much more, having been reconciled, we shall be saved by His life. And not only that, but we also rejoice in God through our Lord Jesus Christ, through whom we have now received the reconciliation.

Therefore, just as through one man sin entered the world, and death through sin, and thus death spread to all men, because all sinned—(For until the law sin was in the world, but sin is not imputed when there is no law. Nevertheless death reigned from Adam to Moses, even over those who had not sinned according to the likeness of the transgression of Adam, who is a type of Him who was to come.

But the free gift is not like the offense. For if by the one man's offense many died, much more the grace of God and the gift by the grace of the one Man, Jesus Christ, abounded to many. And the gift is not like that which came through the one who sinned. For the judgment which came from one offense resulted in condemnation, but the free gift which came from many offenses resulted in justification. For if by the one man's offense death reigned through the one, much more those who receive abundance of grace and of the gift of righteousness will reign in life through the One, Jesus Christ.)

Revelation 13:8
All who dwell on the earth will worship him, whose names have not been written in the Book of Life of the Lamb slain from the foundation of the world.

1 Corinthians 3:8-15

Now he who plants and he who waters are one, and each one will receive his own reward according to his own labor. For we are God's fellow workers; you are God's field, you are God's building. According to the grace of God which was given to me, as a wise master builder I have laid the foundation, and another builds on it. But let each one take heed how he builds on it. For no other foundation can anyone lay than that which is laid, which is Jesus Christ.

Now if anyone builds on this foundation with gold, silver, precious stones, wood, hay, straw, each one's work will become clear; for the Day will declare it, because it will be revealed by fire; and the fire will test each one's work, of what sort it is. If anyone's work which he has built on it endures, he will receive a reward. If anyone's work is burned, he will suffer loss; but he himself will be saved, yet so as through fire.

ℰ 2 ℛ

God's Grace for the Girl with the Giggle

There was trouble in the camp in the desert: the long-awaited and much-anticipated joy of motherhood had not come to pass as purposed, promised or planned. The clock was ticking, things were tense, tempers flared in the tents through hot, endless days and stone-cold, starry nights. Both the stars and the sands mocked the promises. Yet, God was on the move making the impossible possible and the improbable probable through a man and a woman who both laughed at the prospect of parenthood past their prime.

Genesis 18:9-12
Then they said to him, "Where is Sarah your wife?" So he said, "Here, in the tent." And He said, "I will certainly return to you according to the time of life, and behold, Sarah your wife shall have a son." (Sarah was listening in the tent door which was behind him.) Now Abraham and Sarah were old, well advanced in age; and Sarah had passed the age of childbearing. Therefore Sarah laughed within herself, saying,"After I have grown old, shall I have pleasure, my lord being old also?"

Before this, while the husband slept deeply, our grace-giving God made a unilateral and unconditional promise that this old man would become Father Abraham. His beautiful, barren old wife would become Sarah, the mother of many, the mother of kings. Who could have loved them more?

This gorgeous girl with the grandmotherly face received the news with a somewhat inappropriately goofy giggle. Then she denied the denigrating laugh altogether. Both were known to the God who knows all: all He overlooked and all He overcame.

He is the God of loving liberty. What would have happened to this Daughter of Eve if her God was the author of either legalism or license? If He treated her as she deserved? To mock the great God of heaven and earth was no small thing. Men died for less. Grace abounds.

Instead, His life-giving, loving kindness and His grace-granting goodness triumphed over tragedy. The proof was in the pudding, as but a year later the girl who giggled was a mommy who laughed for joy. The One who loved her more than anyone else made wrong choices right and blessed the barren woman with her beautiful boy baby—long after mothers her age were great grandmothers.

Now the sand of the sea and the stars in the sky shouted the gift of God's promise. There would be land for these desert wanderers, there would be bountiful births, there would be blessings for all the nations on earth. There was grace for the Girl with the Giggle while she waited.

Have you ever lost something like Sarah did? Hers was the loss of a dream: status, significance, security and even safety.

As a Daughter of Eve, I have felt cynical in my soul, as I have been in God's Waiting Room longing for prayers and promises to come to pass. Stress facilitates the odd, goofy giggle that feels more like a snort. Faith flounders yet fights fear in those dark nights of the soul when sometimes the only answer is silence. Then hope surfaces with the sure knowledge that nothing is too difficult for God.

God's perspective is quite different from our perspective. He has quite an advantage because He is omniscient: He knows everything. He is omnipresent: He is everywhere all at the same time.

> *Perspective is everything when you are experiencing the challenges of life.*
> —*Joni Eareckson Tada*[1]

It is worth noting that God is also omnipotent: He is all-powerful. He can change things. Sometimes He does. Sometimes He does not. At the age of 90, the Girl with the Giggle got pregnant. Through the baby named "Laughter" (Isaac), her deepest needs were met by our great God of grace.

When our perspective causes us pain, it is prudent to practice the perspective of God by turning to the presence of God as revealed in the Word of God. As a wise professor once told me during a test review, "You would do well to know this." The more knowledge we have, and the more we apply what we know, the more we grow in the wisdom of the Lord. This is a good thing.

MEDITATION

Read these verses silently several times. Highlight with one color the words the Lord said, and use a different color for the words Sarah said. Read the verses out loud.

> ### Genesis 18:13-15
> And the Lord said to Abraham, "Why did Sarah laugh, saying, 'Shall I surely bear a child, since I am old?' Is anything too hard for the Lord? At the appointed time I will return to you, according to the time of life, and Sarah shall have a son." But Sarah denied it, saying, "I did not laugh," for she was afraid. And He said, "No, but you did laugh!"

Application

Think of something that seems too difficult for you. Explain by answering: Who? What? When? Why? Where? or How?

_____

_____

How did God give grace to the Giggler? _____
Is your situation too difficult for God?_____ Is your response too difficult for God? _____

Contemplation

Circle one and explain: How do these verses comfort you? Correct you? Change you? Challenge you? Calm you? _____

_____

_____

Personal Prayer

> **Lord, I thank You that sweet sister Sarah had a son named "Laughter." That causes me to smile. Weeping may endure for a night, but joy comes in the morning. Your grace is enough when silence sears my soul. Nothing is too difficult for You. Amen.**

TEACHING TIP

Get the student into the Bible and get the Bible into the student through personal application. Seeing God's grace for Sarah, a student can look for God's unreasonable kindness in her/his life.

CHAPTER TWO NOTES

THE ABRAHAMIC COVENANT

Read Genesis Chapter 18

Genesis 15:4-8
And behold, the word of the Lord came to him, saying, "This one shall not be your heir, but one who will come from your own body shall be your heir." Then He brought him outside and said, "Look now toward heaven, and count the stars if you are able to number them." And He said to him,"So shall your descendants be." And he believed in the Lord, and He accounted it to him for righteousness. Then He said to him, "I am the Lord, who brought you out of Ur of the Chaldeans, to give you this land to inherit it."

Genesis 15:17-18
And it came to pass, when the sun went down and it was dark, that behold, there appeared a smoking oven and a burning torch that passed between those pieces. On the same day the Lord made a covenant with Abram, saying: "To your descendants I have given this land, from the river of Egypt to the great river, the River Euphrates."

Genesis 22:15-19
Then the Angel of the Lord called to Abraham a second time out of heaven, and said: "By Myself I have sworn, says the Lord, because you have done this thing, and have not withheld your son, your only son—blessing I will bless you, and multiplying I will multiply your descendants as the stars of the heaven and as the sand which is on the seashore; and your descendants shall possess the gate of their enemies. In your seed all the nations of the earth shall be blessed, because you have obeyed My voice." So Abraham returned to his young men, and they rose and went together to Beersheba; and Abraham dwelt at Beersheba.

Jeremiah 32:17
Ah, Lord God! Behold, You have made the heavens and the earth by Your great power and outstretched arm. There is nothing too hard for You.

Psalm 30:5b
Weeping may endure for a night, but joy comes in the morning.

3

God's Grace for the Woman Who Wept by the Water

Through a mysterious and seemingly nefarious set of circumstances, the people of promise came to be in a foreign land, a land not of milk and honey, but one of garlic and leek. There, through the glorious grace of God, they escaped famine. Far from the Fertile Crescent, they multiplied and added to their number, so much so that it caused fear in the heart of the pharaoh. A rigorous rule decreed their babies born boys were to be banished from that land and left to drown in the river Nile.

Exodus 2:1-3
And a man of the house of Levi went and took as wife a daughter of Levi. So the woman conceived and bore a son. And when she saw that he was a beautiful child, she hid him three months. But when she could no longer hide him, she took an ark of bulrushes for him, daubed it with asphalt and pitch, put the child in it, and laid it in the reeds by the river's bank.

An unwritten exception clause that might be called the "halo effect" saved a beautiful boy. A Daughter of Eve, when she could no longer keep her secret silent, hid her baby in a basket, took him to the river, and released him to the goodness of God. Who could have loved her more? Mere moments later, a royal daughter discovered this crying bundle of joy whom her father, the pharaoh, had decreed doomed to death. Love lifted the little child into the arms of this ruling family. Grace was given, and given again when Miriam, the sister of this baby, was right there on the spot, ready to help.

At the scene of divine destiny, in the prologue of the greatest story ever told, the sister of Moses was part of the plan that God put in place, to place the baby in the basket back into his own mother's arms. She was selected by divine design to nurture and nourish the baby she birthed. The Woman who Wept by the Water, no doubt, wept for joy.

A nation was formed by the God of grace, just laws were given to govern, blessings were bestowed, and boundaries on behavior were set in stone. Because our generous God spoke to Moses from the blazing burning bush: men and women were significant, marriage sacred, children safe, mothers secure.

These were the blessings of liberty within the protection of the law. The law was laced with love, but could be distorted by lack of control in the form of license, or cold-hearted compliance manifested as legalism. God loved them, and led them, and set them apart. The woman with the baby in the basket became the mother of the man Moses, who led his people to the longed-for land of promise.

There is nothing more fierce, nor fearsome, than a mother's love for her children. When you release your child to the grace of God, you wait for the God of grace to bring that child back.

Later in time, another parent stood watching and waiting for a son to come home. In that poignant prodigal picture, there is pledge of a party that will one day celebrate a promised return.

As a Daughter of Eve, I watch and wait for that glorious day when God will gather His children together. One day, perhaps today, and for sure on that day: all will be made right.

It is true, and I cannot wait, but I do. In the meantime I look with joy to God's unreasonable kindness for the Woman who Wept by the Water, and for the father who waited at the window. Both were waiting in a place of promise.

Beth Moore speaks of this as your Promised Land, the place where God's personalized promises over your life become a living reality in your life. Theology forms the foundation. Faith transforms the theory into reality. Liberty lives and loves in that land; because the Lord of life reigns in that land, the Land of Promise is our homeland. Grace abounds.

> *Your Promised Land is the place where God's personalized promises over your life become a living reality rather than a theological theory.*
> —**Beth Moore**[1]

MEDITATION

Read several times. Underline words that show God cares.

Exodus 3:14, 15b-16

And God said to Moses, "I AM WHO I AM." And He said, "Thus you shall say to the children of Israel, 'I AM has sent me to you...This is My name forever, and this is My memorial to all generations.' Go and gather the elders of Israel together, and say to them, 'The Lord God of your fathers, the God of Abraham, of Isaac, and of Jacob, appeared to me, saying, 'I have surely visited you and seen what is done to you in Egypt.'"

Application

Describe an event in your life that has caused you to weep by the water or watch at the window for help from God:

_____

_____

In these times, God whispers to you, "I am indeed concerned about you and what has been done to you." Does this apply to you? What does this teach you about God?

_____

How does God show His grace for you in these times?

_____

Contemplation

Circle one and explain: How do these verses comfort you? Correct you? Change you? Challenge you? Calm you?

_____

_____

Personal Prayer

Lord, You are the God of Abraham, Isaac, and Jacob. No one could love me more. When I smile in the sunshine, or weep by the waters of life, You are with me and are concerned about what happens to me. You comfort me because you care for me. Thank You. Amen

TEACHING TIP

Write a note to God thanking Him for His grace to you in a season of weeping or waiting. Read it again when God has shown His concern for you in some specific way. Remember His faithfulness and rejoice.

CHAPTER THREE NOTES

THE MOSAIC COVENANT

Read Deuteronomy 28-29

Blessing: Deuteronomy 28:1-2

"Now it shall come to pass, if you diligently obey the voice of the Lord your God, to observe carefully all His commandments which I command you today, the Lord your God will set you high above all nations of the earth. And all these blessings shall come upon you and overtake you, because you obey the voice of the Lord your God."

Cursing: Deuteronomy 28:15

"But it shall come to pass, if you do not obey the voice of the Lord your God, to observe carefully all His commandments and His statutes which I command you today, that all these curses will come upon you and overtake you."

Conclusion: Deuteronomy 29:9

"Therefore keep the words of this covenant, and do them, that you may prosper in all that you do."

NEW TESTAMENT: GRACE THROUGH FAITH

Ephesians 2:4-10

But God, who is rich in mercy, because of His great love with which He loved us, even when we were dead in trespasses, made us alive together with Christ (by grace you have been saved), and raised us up together, and made us sit together in the heavenly places in Christ Jesus, that in the ages to come He might show the exceeding riches of His grace in His kindness toward us in Christ Jesus. For by grace you have been saved through faith, and that not of yourselves; it is the gift of God, not of works, lest anyone should boast. For we are His workmanship, created in Christ Jesus for good works, which God prepared beforehand that we should walk in them.

Galatians 3:19-4:3

What purpose then does the law serve? It was added because of transgressions, till the Seed should come to whom the promise was made; and it was appointed through angels by the hand of a mediator. Now a mediator does not mediate for one only, but God is one. Is the law then against the promises of God? Certainly not! For if there had been a law given which could have given life, truly righteousness would have been by the law. But the Scripture has confined all under sin, that the promise by faith in Jesus Christ might be given to those who believe. But before faith came, we were kept under guard by the law, kept for the faith which would afterward be revealed.

Therefore the law was our tutor to bring us to Christ, that we might be justified by faith. But after faith has come, we are no longer under a tutor. For you are all sons of God through faith in Christ Jesus. For as many of you as were baptized into Christ have put on Christ. There is neither Jew nor Greek, there is neither slave nor free, there is neither male nor female; for you are all one in Christ Jesus. And if you are Christ's, then you are Abraham's seed, and heirs according to the promise.

Now I say that the heir, as long as he is a child, does not differ at all from a slave, though he is master of all, but is under guardians and stewards until the time appointed by the father.

℘ 4 ℃

God's Grace for the Warrior Woman

T he favored weapons of mass destruction at the time were iron chariots. The enemy had 900 of them. Their leader loomed large over the landscape of the people of the Lord. So what did God do? He called His sitting servant to serve Him. And where was this servant sitting? Right under the Palm Tree of Deborah, where she always sat sorting out the problems of the populace when they came seeking solutions.

She was the mother with the message, the prophetess with the prophecy. She was God's go-to gal, this Daughter of Eve. Deborah went to Barack, aka "Thunder and Lightning," to summon him to arms on a mission of mercy for the people of the Book. Little did he know that while hanging on to that mother's apron strings, it truly would be God's thunder and lightning that would save the day. Grace abounds.

How had it come to this? This particular problem began during the longest period of peace in the Book of Judges: 80 years, to be precise. However there was a predicament. Problems tend to perpetuate themselves, as attitudes turn into behaviors

Judges 4:6a; 8
Then she sent and called for Barak the son of Abinoam from Kedesh in Naphtali, and said to him, "Has not the Lord God of Israel commanded, 'Go and deploy troops at Mount Tabor; take with you ten thousand men'...And Barak said to her, "If you will go with me, then I will go; but if you will not go with me, I will not go!"

that engender consequences. These are ABC's of hapless history. But hope happened under that palm tree, by God's grace and for God's glory.

This is how it worked: because they strayed from the Word, the people, like sheep, would wander from their shepherd. The consequences of their actions left them ensnared, trapped. They then would shout to the Lord to help them. He, of unreasonable kindness, then would save them. Periods of peace would follow, 'til the previous pattern prevailed yet again. To put a fine point on it, there were seven such cycles of Judges. You would think they would learn. Who could have loved them more?

> *True success in any endeavor can only come when the Father has initiated the activity and invited our participation.*
>
> *— Priscilla Shirer[1]*

The Lord, Mighty in Battle, led them to a most peculiar victory. Way up on the mountain, the mother and the men gathered. Way down in the valley, the chariots roared. High in the sky lightning flaunted itself, flagrantly flashing while thunder fearsomely followed.

Right in the middle of the dry season, drenching rain reigned from the God of heaven and earth. Mud sucked at stuck chariots and the men who manned them died. The enemy king escaped to a tent of a kinsman, empty save for the lady of the house. Exhausted, he asked for

> **Judges 5:24-25**
> "Most blessed among women is Jael, the wife of Heber the Kenite; blessed is she among women in tents. He asked for water, she gave milk; she brought out cream in a lordly bowl."

water, got warm milk, conceivably dozed, and died. How had that happened? That lone woman, Jael, nailed him. You could rightly exclaim that he got hammered. The battle was won.

Sometimes it takes us by surprise when God calls upon us to right a wrong. I resist that role. However, there were strange comings and goings in a vacant house on our street. It was unsettling—frightening, in fact. I debated and deliberated, then I documented. One day when the time was right, the authorities gathered up the evidence, and then gathered up the vagrant who had unlawfully settled in to his new home, the home he'd no doubt laughingly, lovingly and longingly decorated with empty fast food wrappers.

Peace returned to me, and to the quiet little corner of my world. Daughters of Eve are pressed into service for the strangest of things. We are often unwilling warriors in a war predicted from the start of time. Grace abounds.

MEDITATION

Read several times, and then ponder the underlined words from
"The Song of Deborah and Barak."

Judges 5:1-3, 21b
Then Deborah and Barak the son of Abinoam <u>sang</u> on that
day, <u>saying</u>: "When leaders <u>lead</u> in Israel, when the people
willingly <u>offer</u> themselves, <u>bless</u> the Lord!" "<u>Hear</u>, O kings!
<u>Give ear</u>, O princes! I, even I, will <u>sing</u> to the Lord; I will
<u>sing</u> praise to the Lord God of Israel...O my soul, <u>march on</u>
in strength!"

Application

If you are called upon to right a wrong, what tools mentioned
above will help you march on with strength in your soul? Explain.

_____

_____

How did God give grace to the Warrior Woman?

_____

Contemplation

Circle one and explain: How do these verses comfort you?
Challenge you? Calm you?

_____

_____

Personal Prayer

Lord, when I feel resistance within myself to follow You,
strengthen my soul; my mind, my will, my emotions.
Remind me to sing praise to You, O Lord. O my soul,
march on with strength. Amen

TEACHING TIP

As a warm-up exercise, before you teach this Meditation, have
students list and discuss obstacles that might hinder change in
their lives. Note that resistance to change can be quite strong,
and very normal.

CHAPTER FOUR NOTES

READ JUDGES CHAPTERS FOUR AND FIVE

Judges 4:6-10
Then she sent and called for Barak the son of Abinoam from Kedesh in Naphtali, and said to him, "Has not the Lord God of Israel commanded, 'Go and deploy troops at Mount Tabor; take with you ten thousand men of the sons of Naphtali and of the sons of Zebulun; and against you I will deploy Sisera, the commander of Jabin's army, with his chariots and his multitude at the River Kishon; and I will deliver him into your hand'?"

And Barak said to her, "If you will go with me, then I will go; but if you will not go with me, I will not go!"

So she said, "I will surely go with you; nevertheless there will be no glory for you in the journey you are taking, for the Lord will sell Sisera into the hand of a woman." Then Deborah arose and went with Barak to Kedesh. And Barak called Zebulun and Naphtali to Kedesh; he went up with ten thousand men under his command, and Deborah went up with him.

Judges 4:14-16
Then, Deborah said to Barak, "Up! For this is the day in which the Lord has delivered Sisera into your hand. Has not the Lord gone out before you?" So Barak went down from Mount Tabor with ten thousand men following him. And the Lord routed Sisera and all his chariots and all his army with the edge of the sword before Barak; and Sisera alighted from his chariot and fled away on foot. But Barak pursued the chariots and the army as far as Harosheth Hagoyim, and all the army of Sisera fell by the edge of the sword; not a man was left.

Judges 5:12
"Awake, awake, Deborah! Awake, awake, sing a song! Arise, Barak, and lead your captives away, O son of Abinoam!"

Judges 5:26-27
She stretched her hand to the tent peg, her right hand to the workmen's hammer; she pounded Sisera, she pierced his head, she split and struck through his temple. At her feet he sank, he fell, he lay still; at her feet he sank, he fell; where he sank, there he fell dead.

Judges 5:31
"Thus let all Your enemies perish, O Lord! But let those who love Him be like the sun when it comes out in full strength." So the land had rest for forty years.

ಖ 5 ಚ

God's Grace for the Widow with Wisdom

W hat do you do with a woman like Abigail? She married into a legendary line of fearless fighters who, generations ago under Caleb, led the people of promise into the Promised Land. Caleb was noble; his decadent descendant Nabal, her husband, was not. His name, meaning "fool," tells the tale. Abigail's churlish spouse was ill-suited to live on the hereditary badlands near the wilderness by Hebron and Carmel. No fighter was he out on that frontier, preferring instead the cozy comforts his wealth bought.

Nearby, outlaws marauded, foraging for food, stealing sheep. Sheep? Well, ignoble Nabal had thousands of them, and hundreds of goats, as well. No one ever need go hungry in that neck of the woods. For some time all was quiet on that southern front because a shepherd-warrior named David protected Nabal's flocks with a wall of men, over 400 fighters strong. Never, not once, did David's crew steal a single lamb chop for dinner.

> *Courage is not simply one of the virtues, but the form of every virtue at the testing point.*
> **—C. S. Lewis**[1]

But as their supplies ran dangerously low, they asked Nabal for food. Unhappily, this fool in his folly, responded with, "Who is David?" Seriously. He did. He flatly refused their request. In the land where hospitality was king, this man who was just barely sovereign over sheep would not help the man who helped him. You can only imagine David's response. He promptly made a vow to destroy this mad man.

But, what of Abigail? This, after all, is her story. God had a plan for her that may have seemed highly irregular. Her story is history, included in sacred writ, instructive to Daughters of Eve. Long ago, way back in the beginning, God Himself spoke the words, "It is not good for man to be alone: I will make him a helper suitable for him" (Gen. 2:18). With those words God revealed what He was up to with Eve, and many Daughters of Eve to follow.

Nabal needed help. God gave him a helper named Abigail, a woman of courage. What a wife she was. She was beautiful to behold, winsome in word and deed, wise in the ways life works. When she heard of her husband's cruel and callous rebuff to the request of David, she immediately had helpers load donkeys with exorbitant gifts of customary hospitality, including bushels of bread, bags of roasted grain, baskets of cakes, barrels of wine, and five roasted sheep.

Sending the supplies ahead of her, off she rode on her donkey, all alone deep down a draw in the Judean wilderness, on a divine mission of mercy. Abigail did this without the knowledge of her husband, but within her wiring was woven the mysterious mandate to help her husband. Surely, this was not her first rodeo.

Who could have known, except the Lord, that David was dashing through the darkness that very moment, with 400 sword-bearing soldiers to avenge the wrong Nabal had done? No harm, no foul. God is a shield and a shelter in time of need. When the choice for a godly woman is either to surrender to evil or be obedient to God, God trumps and God triumphs.

> **1 Samuel 25:32-33, 35**
> Then David said to Abigail: "Blessed is the Lord God of Israel, who sent you this day to meet me! And blessed is your advice and blessed are you, because you have kept me this day from coming to bloodshed and from avenging myself with my own hand. "So David received from her hand what she had brought him, and said to her, "Go up in peace to your house. See, I have heeded your voice and respected your person."

Abigail returned home to find the annual traditional sheep-shearing festivities under way; this one was fit for a king. The Sheep Sovereign was well into his cups. This wise woman, not yet a widow, waited until morning to tell of the death and destruction Nabal had narrowly missed. His heart became like stone; ten days later he died. Guess what? David proposed and promptly married the winsome Widow with Wisdom. Abigail lived in Hebron with David, where he became the King of Judah. Later she moved to Jerusalem with him when he was King of all Israel. Who could have loved her more but God?

As a Daughter of Eve, I reflect on Abigail's dilemma. If she had deferred to her husband's decision, she would have enabled evil. Instead, this godly woman looked to the Lord for deliverance and He included her in the solution. Each individual is personally accountable to God for the choices they make. License ignores it, legalism wants to supervise it, but liberty requires it. God's grace is truly amazing.

MEDITATION

Read the following text several times. Underline the words know and consider.

> **1 Samuel 25:17a**
> "Now therefore, know and consider what you will do, for harm is determined against our master and against all his household. For he is such a scoundrel that one cannot speak to him."

Application

When faced with a problem, what are the first two things you should do before you do anything else? How does this apply to you?

_____

_____

Abigail acted quickly, but thoughtfully. Nabal reacted impulsively. What difference did it make?

_____

When did God give grace to Abigail?

_____

Contemplation

Circle one and explain: How do these verses comfort you? Correct you? Change you? Challenge you? Calm you?

_____

_____

Personal Prayer

Lord, help me to react to problems in my life the way Abigail did. I want to think and consider what to do. Help me then to do it. Amen

TEACHING TIP

Read the rest of the story: So when David heard that Nabal was dead, he said, "Blessed be the Lord, who has pleaded the cause of my reproach from the hand of Nabal, and has kept His servant from evil! For the Lord has returned the wickedness of Nabal on his own head." And David sent and proposed to Abigail, to take her as his wife.
(1 Samuel 25:39-40)

CHAPTER FIVE NOTES

READ 1 SAMUEL 25.

1 Samuel 25:2-14

Now there was a man in Maon whose business was in Carmel, and the man was very rich. He had three thousand sheep and a thousand goats. And he was shearing his sheep in Carmel. The name of the man was Nabal, and the name of his wife Abigail. And she was a woman of good understanding and beautiful appearance; but the man was harsh and evil in his doings. He was of the house of Caleb.

When David heard in the wilderness that Nabal was shearing his sheep, David sent ten young men; and David said to the young men, "Go up to Carmel, go to Nabal, and greet him in my name. And thus you shall say to him who lives in prosperity: 'Peace be to you, peace to your house, and peace to all that you have! Now I have heard that you have shearers. Your shepherds were with us, and we did not hurt them, nor was there anything missing from them all the while they were in Carmel. Ask your young men, and they will tell you. Therefore let my young men find favor in your eyes, for we come on a feast day. Please give whatever comes to your hand to your servants and to your son David.'"

So when David's young men came, they spoke to Nabal according to all these words in the name of David, and waited. Then Nabal answered David's servants, and said, "Who is David, and who is the son of Jesse? There are many servants nowadays who break away each one from his master. Shall I then take my bread and my water and my meat that I have killed for my shearers, and give it to men when I do not know where they are from?"

So David's young men turned on their heels and went back; and they came and told him all these words. Then David said to his men, "Every man gird on his sword." So every man girded on his sword, and David also girded on his sword. And about four hundred men went with David, and two hundred stayed with the supplies.

Psalm 91:4

He shall cover you with His feathers, and under His wings you shall take refuge; His truth shall be your shield and buckler.

Ezekiel 18:19-20

Yet you say, 'Why should the son not bear the guilt of the father?' Because the son has done what is lawful and right, and has kept all My statutes and observed them, he shall surely live. The soul who sins shall die. The son shall not bear the guilt of the father, nor the father bear the guilt of the son. The righteousness of the righteous shall be upon himself, and the wickedness of the wicked shall be upon himself.

God's Grace for the Girl Next Door

T
he time of the kings had come to the land, and in the season of the year when men went out to war, a young king stayed cloistered in his castle. This wondrous warrior was known far and wide as the Giant Killer. However, he was not where giants were being killed that day. In fact, in the dark of that night, the king restlessly roamed the roof of his residence where, lo and behold, he beheld the bathing of the beautiful Bathsheba, the Girl Next Door.

> **2 Samuel 11:1a; 1c, 2, 4-5**
> It happened in the spring of the year, at the time when kings go out to battle... David remained at Jerusalem. Then it happened one evening that David arose from his bed and walked on the roof of the king's house. And from the roof he saw a woman bathing, and the woman was very beautiful to behold.... Then David sent messengers, and took her; and she came to him, and he lay with her, for she was cleansed from her impurity; and she returned to her house. And the woman conceived; so she sent and told David, and said, "I am with child."

She was already wed to a warrior who actually went to war. Through a series of suspect, but not secret, circumstances, David bedded then later wedded the weeping widow whose husband was fatally injured in battle.

When her baby died, she cried. David comforted the mourning mother, and love's gift was a second son, Solomon, who one day would be king. Through these tragic turning points of Bathsheba's life, the Lord sent the prophet Nathan to sustain her, and through Bathsheba, God's gracious plan was perfected. Who could have loved her more?

As the wind whispered under the stars in the sky, and over the sand by the sea, perhaps creation groaned in anticipation that promises made in the garden, on the desert, from the mountain, and rather recently in the fields to David-a shepherd boy- might be fully fulfilled by our God of unreasonable kindness.

In due season David, aka the Dancing King, became a dying old man. Succession for the second son had been the promise to the mother, but this became a problem because another was about to seize the throne instead. Bathsheba, this Daughter of Eve, entered the king's chambers and reminded her beloved husband of his words to her so long ago: "Surely your son Solomon shall be king after me and he shall sit on my throne" (I Kings 1:17).

> *God chose David. On the surface, the choice made no sense. But God doesn't work on sense; He works on grace. God called you, and God called me. He knew what He was doing.*
> —**Beth Moore**[1]

Through their line the promises of God were fulfilled beyond their wildest dreams. Some choices make no sense from the human vantage point, but are perfectly placed and positioned from God's view. When life began to leave the king, the Girl Next Door became the Queen Mother of the land of promise. Grace was given, and given again.

From the start, God's right to rule and reign over His creation was questioned as doubt slithered and stalked through the

Garden at the end of the beginning. The classic question of all time is the theodicy: "How could a good and loving God allow... any number of things?" Bathsheba might have put it this way: "How could a good and loving God allow my first baby to die?"

Questions pop up unbidden about a seemingly untimely death, a sudden sickness, an unexpected natural disaster, or a tragic accident. Sometimes God uses strength to accomplish His will; often He uses weakness. Suffering comes in many shapes and sizes and is often the companion of change.

The ups and downs of marriage, the ins and outs of children, the stops and starts of friendships: as a Daughter of Eve, these cause me pause. But when I was diagnosed with cancer, these ambivalent and free-floating wonderings came sharply into focus. So, the real question behind the theodicy is actually three-fold: Is God good? Is God loving? Is God, God?

My conclusion: God is, and is good. Everything that touches my life is filtered through His lavish love for me. The One who loves me more is always there for me, just as He was for the Girl Next Door. One glorious day at the beginning of forever, the veil will be lifted and we will see Jesus face to face, one day. On that day we will see Him as both rewarder and redeemer. Faith grows and grace abounds.

MEDITATION

Read the following prayer written by the husband of the girl next door. Hear his heart.

Psalm 51:1-2
Have mercy upon me, O God, according to Your lovingkindness; according to the multitude of Your tender mercies, blot out my transgressions. Wash me thoroughly from my iniquity, and cleanse me from my sin.

Application

Circle words or phrases that indicate David was teachable. Underline words that indicate David's tendency toward tenderness. How might these attitudes have affected Bathsheba in her marriage to David?

_____

_____

How did God give grace to the Girl Next Door?

_____

Contemplation

Circle one and explain: How do these verses comfort you? Correct you? Change you? Challenge you? Calm you?

_____

_____

Personal Prayer

O God, because your love never fails, I can ask you to have mercy on me: wash me, purify me and relieve my guilt. Restore to me the joy of your salvation. Help me to be willing to obey you. Amen.

TEACHING TIP

When reading Scripture like this portion of Psalm 51, notice the personal pronouns (*me, my* and *I*) in David's prayer. Read it again as though it is the prayer of your own heart. Did you notice that your mind, will and emotions are involved? This is called active learning.

CHAPTER SIX NOTES

THE DAVIDIC COVENANT

Read 2 Samuel 7:1-29

2 Samuel 7:8-17

Now therefore, thus shall you say to My servant David, 'Thus says the Lord of hosts: "I took you from the sheepfold, from following the sheep, to be ruler over My people, over Israel. And I have been with you wherever you have gone, and have cut off all your enemies from before you, and have made you a great name, like the name of the great men who are on the earth.

Moreover I will appoint a place for My people Israel, and will plant them, that they may dwell in a place of their own and move no more; nor shall the sons of wickedness oppress them anymore, as previously, since the time that I commanded judges to be over My people Israel, and have caused you to rest from all your enemies. Also the Lord tells you that He will make you a house.'"

"When your days are fulfilled and you rest with your fathers, I will set up your seed after you, who will come from your body, and I will establish his kingdom. He shall build a house for My name, and I will establish the throne of his kingdom forever. I will be his Father, and he shall be My son. If he commits iniquity, I will chasten him with the rod of men and with the blows of the sons of men.

But My mercy shall not depart from him, as I took it from Saul, whom I removed from before you, and your house and your kingdom shall be established forever before you. Your throne shall be established forever.'" According to all these words and according to all this vision, so Nathan spoke to David.

Psalm 23

The Lord is my shepherd;I shall not want. He makes me to lie down in green pastures; He leads me beside the still waters. He restores my soul; He leads me in the paths of righteousness for His name's sake. Yea, though I walk through the valley of the shadow of death, I will fear no evil; for You are with me;Your rod and Your staff, they comfort me. You prepare a table before me in the presence of my enemies; You anoint my head with oil; My cup runs over. Surely goodness and mercy shall follow me all the days of my life; and I will dwell in the house of the Lord forever.

Hebrews 11:6
But without faith it is impossible to please Him, for he who comes to God must believe that He is, and that He is a rewarder of those who diligently seek Him.

2 Samuel 12:24-25
Then David comforted Bathsheba his wife, and went in to her and lay with her. So she bore a son, and he called his name Solomon. Now the Lord loved him.

1 Kings 1:28-30
Then King David answered and said, "Call Bathsheba to me." So she came into the king's presence and stood before the king. And the king took an oath and said, "As the Lord lives, who has redeemed my life from every distress, just as I swore to you by the Lord God of Israel, saying, 'Assuredly Solomon your son shall be king after me, and he shall sit on my throne in my place,' so I certainly will do this day."

ഇ 7 ര

God's Grace for the Wife That Never Was

I t could be said that it all began in the womb of the mother of Jeremiah, but in reality it began in the mind of God long before then. Some are set aside for secular service, some for sacred service. Both are high and holy callings. The latter was the life for Jeremiah. He could have been quite a catch—he was a prophet born into a prominent priestly family.

But he was a man of promise with a problem. He would go on to protect the kingly line of David, but as for Jeremiah, his line would never begin. No long lists of loved ones would be written in his obituary. From Jeremiah's call to Jerusalem's fall, this man's mission required such single-sightedness that singleness was the requisite.

God Himself said that it was not good for man to be alone, but in God's great wisdom, the weeping prophet wept alone. People, priests

Jeremiah 16:1-2
The word of the Lord also came to me, saying, "You shall not take a wife, nor shall you have sons or daughters in this place."

and prophets wanted to put him to death. The wife he never had was spared a life of danger, dread and disease. Sometimes, there are dreams that are never realized and prayers are seemingly unanswered as life takes its twisted turns. Yet, grace abounds.

He lived in turbulent times: kings and kingdoms came and went but not without great struggles. War was wild and widespread. Words from this prophet were whispered warnings from God, encouraging and exhorting His people to come back to Him. Who could have loved them more?

At that time, the people of the Promised Land lived in the land promised to Abraham and were ruled by a good king. There was just one particular thing missing, and perhaps no one even knew it was gone. But gone it was. The Law had been lost. Their culture looked just like the pagan cultures that pressed in on them from every side. Blessings eluded them because they had not learned the lost Law written in stone: that gracious love letter from the lover of their souls. God brought it, Moses taught it, but people forgot it.

One day it happened: the Book of the Law was found by Jeremiah's own father. Promises were renewed, the temple temporarily restored, and Passover reinstated. Hope had a heyday as it bubbled up through parched hearts: dried, discouraged, and dejected through years of rebellion.

Though there was delight in this season, it was short-lived because their good king was killed in battle. Three waves of deportation took them far from their lovely land. Jeremiah stood on the crossroads of history, a man without a country, a man without a family, a man who lost all but gained everything.

> *"Love is not patronizing and charity isn't about pity, it is about love. Charity and love are the same."*
> —**Mother Teresa**[1]

In Jeremiah's lifetime he was the man who never married the Wife That Never Was. But think about this: if God considered Himself the husband to the people of promise, then astonishingly and

44

astoundingly, it could be said that God Himself had entrusted His beloved bride, His Israel, to Jeremiah to love, feed, lead and protect. Even in those dark and despairing times, the Lord's unreasonable kindness shone brightly.

God told Jeremiah that there would come a day when the external influence of God would become an internal reality. Imagine that: the Lord would personally write His law in the hearts of His people. He would educate, exhort and encourage, from the inside out. Who knew ... this would truly be a new covenant!

Jeremiah 31:33
But this is the covenant that I will make with the house of Israel after those days, says the Lord: I will put My law in their minds, and write it on their hearts; and I will be their God, and they shall be My people.

Unlike the Wife That Never Was, I am the wife who is, for over 50 years. I live in a time Jeremiah could only dream of. Though not fully actualized, that New Covenant makes it possible for me, and for my husband, to listen to the words God has written in our hearts through His Holy Spirit, who comforts us, corrects us, changes us, challenges us, and calms us, just when we need it. Imagine that!

MEDITATION

Read several times. Look for a list in this text.

Jeremiah 29:11-14a

For I know the thoughts that I think toward you, says the Lord, thoughts of peace and not of evil, to give you a future and a hope. Then you will call upon Me and go and pray to Me, and I will listen to you, and you will seek Me and find Me, when you search for Me with all your heart. I will be found by you, says the Lord, and I will bring you back from your captivity.

Application

When life takes its twisted turns, it is easy to feel like the Wife That Never Was. When great and good plans collapse, it is possible to crumble with them. Hope is helped by God's unreasonable kindness. God's plans include three things according to the first sentence of Jeremiah 29:11:

1. _____   2. _____   3. _____

Read your part in this process and memorize it:

1. Call upon God. 2. Come to God. 3. Pray to God. 4. Seek God.

5. Search for God with all of your heart. 6. Find God.

Contemplation

Circle one and explain: How do these verses comfort you? Correct you? Change you? Challenge you? Calm you?

_____

_____

Personal Prayer

Lord, I know your plans for me are good, they give me a future and hope. Knowing that, I call upon You, I come to You, I pray to You. Thank You for listening to me, thank You that I can find You, because You are actually calling me to You. Amen

TEACHING TIP

Have each student turn to someone and say what she or he learned. Have the other person restate what she or he heard. Repeat the process. They will probably learn something you did not teach them.

CHAPTER SEVEN NOTES

Genesis 2:18-19
And the Lord God said, "It is not good that man should be alone; I will make him a helper comparable to him."

Jeremiah 1:5
"Before I formed you in the womb I knew you; before you were born I sanctified you; I ordained you a prophet to the nations."

THE NEW COVENANT

Jeremiah 31:31-34
"Behold, the days are coming, says the Lord, when I will make a new covenant with the house of Israel and with the house of Judah — not according to the covenant that I made with their fathers in the day that I took them by the hand to lead them out of the land of Egypt, My covenant which they broke, though I was a husband to them, says the Lord. But this is the covenant that I will make with the house of Israel after those days, says the Lord: I will put My law in their minds, and write it on their hearts; and I will be their God, and they shall be My people. No more shall every man teach his neighbor, and every man his brother, saying, 'Know the Lord,' for they all shall know Me, from the least of them to the greatest of them, says the Lord. For I will forgive their iniquity, and their sin I will remember no more."

Luke 22:20
Likewise He also took the cup after supper, saying, "This cup is the new covenant in My blood, which is shed for you."

2 Corinthians 3:2-11
You are our epistle written in our hearts, known and read by all men; clearly you are an epistle of Christ, ministered by us, written not with ink but by the Spirit of the living God, not on tablets of stone but on tablets of flesh, that is, of the heart.

And we have such trust through Christ toward God. Not that we are sufficient of ourselves to think of anything as being from ourselves, but our sufficiency is from God, who also made us sufficient as ministers of the new covenant, not of the letter but of the Spirit; for the letter kills, but the Spirit gives life.

But if the ministry of death, written and engraved on stones, was glorious, so that the children of Israel could not look steadily at the face of Moses because of the glory of his countenance, which glory was passing away, how will the ministry of the Spirit not be more glorious? For if the ministry of condemnation had glory, the ministry of righteousness exceeds much more in glory. For even what was made glorious had no glory in this respect, because of the glory that excels. For if what is passing away was glorious, what remains is much more glorious.

Hebrews 8:8-12

Because finding fault with them, He says: "Behold, the days are coming, says the Lord, when I will make a new covenant with the house of Israel and with the house of Judah — not according to the covenant that I made with their fathers in the day when I took them by the hand to lead them out of the land of Egypt; because they did not continue in My covenant, and I disregarded them, says the Lord. For this is the covenant that I will make with the house of Israel after those days, says the Lord: I will put My laws in their mind and write them on their hearts; and I will be their God, and they shall be My people. None of them shall teach his neighbor, and none his brother, saying, 'Know the Lord,' for all shall know Me, from the least of them to the greatest of them. For I will be merciful to their unrighteousness, and their sins and their lawless deeds I will remember no more."

ᔆᴐ 8 ᔆᴐ

God's Grace for the Momma by the Manger

Angels were everywhere. Gabriel, in particular, was quite busy with his messages of comfort and compassion from our God of unreasonable kindness. This angel described himself as, "Gabriel, who stands in the presence of God." He seemed to appear when things were dreadfully and desperately discouraging.

Long ago, he had comforted Daniel with the promise and hope of the coming Messiah. Centuries later, Zacharias, Joseph and Mary all received angelic messages within a matter of months. Zacharias was speechless, Joseph was fearless, and Mary, well, she was joyous.

Prayers and promises from the start of time were about to be realized, in time. Something that had never happened was about to happen at just the right time. All was ready for the birth of the long-awaited, much-anticipated Baby of Bethlehem. Grace abounds.

> **Luke 1:46-47**
> And Mary said:
> "My soul magnifies the Lord, and my spirit has rejoiced in God my Savior."

> *There is nothing at all that God won't forgive.*
> —*Anne Graham Lotz*[1]

Everything was in place when the last piece of the puzzle arrived in Bethlehem on the back of a donkey. Because of a decree by Augustus, taxes were levied and travel was required to hereditary homelands. Roman roads were safe, the Greek language had spread, and there was a definite, but fragile, governmental stability. All of this God prepared in wild anticipation of the birth of His only begotten Son during those screaming, but seemingly silent, 400 years.

This was all part of the sovereign decree of God which began before the Garden. Daughters of Eve, like Sarah, Jochebed, and Bathsheba, were part of the plan. Some might say that none of these women would have been worthy of the high and holy honors God bestowed upon them, but they are a perfect picture of God's grace in action. They were blessed beyond measure by our giving God, just because He loved them.

The time and the line of the Savior was rapidly reaching the moment that the celestial birthday party was about to begin. You would expect something quite spectacular, and so it was. An angel quite accidentally terrified shepherds keeping watch over their flocks that very night.

Fortunately they settled down, because just then a huge heavenly host said, "Glory to God in the highest!" Then, in the dead of night—there was dead silence. Having been told by the angel where to find the focus of all of this celebration, off the shepherds walked to become the first guests to arrive at the party. There they saw God's Good News all bundled up in a blanket: Jesus Christ the Lord.

There had been no baby shower for our dear Mary, no little outfits, no mom cheering her on, no midwife, no proper birthing room: nothing. There was almost no wedding. But God was with Mary, and her husband was with Mary when she brought forth her firstborn Son, our Savior, Emmanuel: "God with us." Jesus was God's great gift of grace to Mary, and to the world.

Other gifts were on the way. Angels were not the only amazing sights in the sky that night. There was a seriously strange star. Wise men followed it to Jesus. They arrived loaded with magnificent gifts fit for a King. It made perfect sense, because Jesus was of the line of David through which came the promise of a King and a Kingdom that would never end. Who could have loved them more?

As a Daughter of Eve, I wonder what it would be like to hear an angel speak. But better yet, God is with us, His Son saves us, His Spirit seals us, and His Word sustains us, because Jesus loves us. His name is more excellent than that of any angel: He is Wonderful, Counselor, Mighty God, Everlasting Father and Prince of Peace.

MEDITATION

Read several times. Underline four things an angel told Joseph in this passage.

Matthew 1:20b-21 and Luke 1:30

An angel of the Lord appeared to him in a dream, saying, "Joseph, son of David, do not be afraid to take to you Mary your wife, for that which is conceived in her is of the Holy Spirit, and she will bring forth a Son, and you shall call His name Jesus, for He will save His people from their sins."...Then the angel said to her, "Do not be afraid, Mary, for you have found favor with God."

Circle the emotion Mary and Joseph have in common.

Application

What did an angel tell the Momma by the Manger?

_____

After these encouraging messages Joseph became fearless and Mary became joyous. Being obedient to God can change a person's feelings. How can this help you when you are afraid?

_____

_____

Hebrews 1 teaches that in these last days God has spoken to us in His Son, Jesus. How does Jesus speak to you?

_____

_____

How does that reveal God's grace to you?

_____

Contemplation

Circle one and explain: How do these verses comfort you?
Correct you? Change you? Challenge you? Calm you?

Personal Prayer

**Lord, when we are afraid, we long to hear from You.
Speak to us through Your Word. Comfort us. Encourage
us. Amen**

TEACHING TIP

Encourage your students to meditate on the names of Jesus,
including Wonderful, Counselor, Mighty God, Everlasting Father
and Prince of Peace.

CHAPTER EIGHT NOTES

Luke 1:46-50
And Mary said: "My soul magnifies the Lord, and my spirit has rejoiced in God my Savior. For He has regarded the lowly state of His maidservant; for behold, henceforth all generations will call me blessed, for He who is mighty has done great things for me, and holy is His name, and His mercy is on those who fear Him from generation to generation.

Luke 2:10-11
Then the angel said to them, "Do not be afraid, for behold, I bring you good tidings of great joy which will be to all people. For there is born to you this day in the city of David a Savior, who is Christ the Lord."

Hebrews 1-4
God, who at various times and in various ways spoke in time past to the fathers by the prophets, has in these last days spoken to us by His Son, whom He has appointed heir of all things, through whom also He made the worlds; who being the brightness of His glory and the express image of His person, and upholding all things by the word of His power, when He had by Himself purged our sins, sat down at the right hand of the Majesty on high, having become so much better than the angels, as He has by inheritance obtained a more excellent name than they.

Isaiah 9:6-8
For unto us a Child is born,
Unto us a Son is given;
And the government will be upon His shoulder.
And His name will be called
Wonderful, Counselor, Mighty God,
Everlasting Father, Prince of Peace.
Of the increase of His government and peace
There will be no end,
Upon the throne of David and over His kingdom,
To order it and establish it with judgment and justice
From that time forward, even forever.
The zeal of the Lord of hosts will perform this.

ဆ 9 ൸

God's Grace for the Mother of the Man

Remember the celestial celebration at the birth of the Christ Child in Bethlehem—the glory, guests, and gifts? Almost immediately after His birth, his parents whisked Jesus off to Egypt to protect him from a crazed, cruel king. When this mad monarch perished, his threats to Jesus died with him. All was quiet in the land they had left, so that small family came home to Israel.

The next recorded event in the life of Jesus happened when He was just 12 years old. The family had gone to Jerusalem to celebrate another homecoming: Passover. As you might recall, Passover was an important Jewish Feast that marked God's extraordinary deliverance of His people from slavery in Egypt-to the land of Israel.

Now, the festival was over and it was time for thousands of folks to travel home. Somehow in the commotion of the caravan; the crowd, the children, the clamor, Jesus was MIA: gone. Mother Mary was not a hovering helicopter mom, micro- managing her first-born's every move. Even so, she realized she'd rather lost track of Jesus on that dusty road toward Nazareth.

Luke 2:48-49

So when they saw Him, they were amazed; and His mother said to Him, "Son, why have You done this to us? Look, Your father and I have sought You anxiously." And He said to them, "Why did you seek Me? Did you not know thatI must be about My Father's business?"

It was easy to understand; no doubt Mary had her hands full with other children. Mother was frantic as she and Joseph followed their footsteps back to Jerusalem, city of Salem, place of peace. There was no peace in that mother's heart as she hurried along, harried and carried by her fears and perhaps her tears. Had Mary lost the Child whom God had entrusted to her?

Three days later they found him. Three days! Jesus was teaching the teachers in the Temple. But all was not well. It was awkward. No matter, something had to be said.

Blended families can be complicated. Mary was His mother; God was His Father—Jesus honored both. In this we see the tension of the hypostatic union: human and divine. He humbled Himself and went home with Mary and Joseph. This emptying is called the kenosis. Scripture is strangely silent on this but throughout His life on earth this Man, who would be King, lived the life of a servant.

Many years later Mary was helping with the festivities at a wedding in Cana, and truth be told she had never actually had a big wedding. A marriage, to be sure, but not an impressive celebration. This gathering was to be splendid and special, particularly for her because her son, Jesus, and His disciples were guests. How much fun was that? It was, until the wine ran out.

Quietly and quickly Mary told Jesus. He knew His time was not yet, so he softly and swiftly asked servants to fill the stone water pots. They did: to the brim. Lo and behold, those six pots-with

"Most important of all, rely moment by moment on Jesus."
—*Gigi Graham Tchividjian[1]*

at least 20 gallons of water each now miraculously contained gallons of noteworthy wedding wine. Jesus poured out grace at that gathering. He honored his mother. There was a certain celebratory ring to it. Who could have loved her more?

This first miracle privately launched the public ministry of Jesus, the Messiah. There was some question as to why the better wine had not been served first, as was customary. Almost no one knew the answer. Perhaps the greatest impact of this sign was upon the disciples. It is written, "This beginning of His signs Jesus did in Cana of Galilee, and manifested His glory; and His disciples believed in Him" (John 2:11). They believed! In Him. What a blessing of grace.

As a Daughter of Eve, I think about this Son's relationship to his mother. Jesus honored His parents. Grown-up sons and daughters who honor their mothers and fathers are grand pictures of God's grace in action. I am blessed by my beloved children, now parents themselves, when they honor their dad and me.

MEDITATION

As you read this Scripture, underline the promise. Think of the implications for your life.

Ephesians 6:2-3
"Honor your father and mother," which is the first commandment with promise: "that it may be well with you and you may live long on the earth."

Application

As an instrument of God's grace to your parents, what would this look like to you? To them?

_____

_____

How did Jesus give grace to His mother in the Temple? At the Wedding of Cana?

_____

But wait: there's more. As Jesus was dying on the cross, He saw His mother and gave her into the safekeeping of His beloved disciple, John. Jesus said just a few more words, then He died (John 19:26-30). How did Jesus give His glorious grace to His mother at Calvary?

_____

_____

Contemplation

Circle one and explain: How do these verses comfort you? Correct you? Change you? Challenge you? Calm you?

_____

_____

Personal Prayer

Lord, help us to be grand examples of Your grace in
action, as we honor our parents. Amen.

TEACHING TIP

What obstacles make this difficult for you to put into practice?

CHAPTER NINE NOTES

Luke 2:46-3:1
Now so it was that after three days they found Him in the temple, sitting in the midst of the teachers, both listening to them and asking them questions, and all who heard Him were astonished at His understanding and answers. So when they saw Him, they were amazed; and His mother said to Him, "Son, why have You done this to us? Look, your father and I have sought You anxiously."

And He said to them, "Why did you seek Me? Did you not know that I must be about My Father's business?" But they did not understand the statement which He spoke to them. Then He went down with them and came to Nazareth, and was subject to them, but His mother kept all these things in her heart, and Jesus increased in wisdom and stature, and in favor with God and men.

Matthew 13:53-57
Now it came to pass, when Jesus had finished these parables, that He departed from there. When He had come to His own country, He taught them in their synagogue, so that they were astonished and said, "Where did this Man get this wisdom and these mighty works? Is this not the carpenter's son? Is not His mother called Mary? And His brothers James, Joses, Simon, and Judas? And His sisters, are they not all with us? Where then did this Man get all these things?" So they were offended at Him.

Matthew 15:1-7
Then the scribes and Pharisees who were from Jerusalem came to Jesus, saying, "Why do Your disciples transgress the tradition of the elders? For they do not wash their hands when they eat bread."

He answered and said to them, "Why do you also transgress the commandment of God because of your tradition? For God commanded, saying, 'Honor your father and your mother'; and, 'He who curses father or mother, let him be put to death.' But you say, 'Whoever says to his father or mother, "Whatever profit you might have received from me is a gift to God" —then he need not honor his father or mother.' Thus you have made the commandment of God of no effect by your tradition. Hypocrites!

John 19:25a-27

Now there stood by the cross of Jesus His mother. When Jesus therefore saw His mother, and the disciple whom He loved standing by, He said to His mother, "Woman, behold your son!" Then He said to the disciple, "Behold your mother!" And from that hour that disciple took her to his own home.

Luke 23:46

And when Jesus had cried out with a loud voice, He said, "Father, 'into Your hands I commit My spirit.'" Having said this, He breathed His last.

God's Grace for the Well Woman

When women went to the water well together, you could have heard their laughter and chatter way before you saw them. But there was a Samaritan woman who went alone. What kind of woman would do that: a prostitute, a beggar, or a wife? It would seem she was none of these. As she neared the well, she saw a stranger who wanted a drink of water.

Instead of water she handed Him three quick questions. A robust theological discussion ensued. When all was said and done, Jesus offered this Samaritan woman water, living water. But then, he made an odd request, "Go call your husband" (John 4:16).

> **John 4:17-19**
> The woman answered and said I have no husband." Jesus said to her, "You have well said, 'I have no husband, for you have had five husbands, and the one whom you now have is not your husband; in that you spoke truly." The woman said to Him, "Sir, I perceive that You are a prophet."

Wouldn't you have been slightly unsettled having a personal discussion with an outsider—out in the middle of nowhere? It's not like she could pick up her cell phone and actually call her husband. If truth be known, and it was, she didn't even currently have a husband! But she'd had five. How could this woman go through five husbands? Death? Divorce? Disease?

She was unsinkable. This bold, bright, brave woman was a quick study, and she asked yet another theological question. You might know that *theology* basically means, "The study of God." She thought this man Jesus was a prophet. What could be better than talking with an actual prophet? Better still would be talking with God incarnate, and so she was.

To complicate matters further, there was a certain cultural animosity going back hundreds of years. Let it suffice to say that when Jewish people came back to Israel after their Babylonian captivity, they came to rebuild their temple. Samaritans wanted to help but were summarily dismissed from the project. So, they built their own temple on nearby Mount Gerizim.

She must have been wondering about worship, because that was the very next thing to pop out of her mouth. This woman was a curious sort to be sure, but of everything she might have had issues with, why this? The first time Jesus ever spoke about true worship was with this Gentile woman. Neither legalism nor license hindered this conversation. Who could have loved her more?

Jesus said, "But an hour is coming, and now is, when the true worshippers shall worship the Father in spirit and truth; for such people the Father seeks to be His worshippers" (John 4:23). See the irony? Jesus sought her. Grace abounds.

She said, "I know that Messiah is coming;when that One comes, He will declare all things to us" (John 4:25). Jesus replied, "I who speak to you am He" (John 4:26). Did you notice that Jesus exerted the full force of His divinity by equating Himself to the Father? This is how He did that: Samaritans studied from the

Pentateuch, the first five books of Moses. By referencing the "I AM" in her Bible, Jesus connected the dots and said, "I… AM *He*."

His disciples were scandalized when they returned from town and saw Jesus talking to a woman, a Samaritan. No one said a word; in fact, you could have heard a water pot drop.

As a Daughter of Eve, I am quite taken by this encounter. To put a very fine point on it, God's grace breaks with tradition. Jesus waited at the well and spoke privately to the woman. Jesus gave unreasonable kindness to this very inquisitive and inquiring woman. He talked to her one-on-one: unheard of at that time and in that place. With her questions answered, she brought the men she knew to Jesus. Is this called Missionary Dating?

> **Exodus 3:14**
> And God said to Moses, "I AM WHO I AM." And He said, "Thus you shall say to the children of Israel, 'I AM has sent me to you.'"

MEDITATION

Read several times and then underline *drinks, water, thirst,* and *well.*

John 4:13-14
Jesus answered and said to her, "Whoever drinks of this water will thirst again, but whoever drinks of the water that I shall give him will never thirst. But the water that I shall give him will become in him a fountain of water springing up into everlasting life."

Application

Restate the main idea using the words you underlined:

_____

_____

How do you see God's amazing grace in action toward this Well Woman?

_____

_____

Contemplation

Circle one and explain: How do these verses comfort you? Correct you? Change you? Challenge you? Calm you?

_____

_____

Personal Prayer

Lord, what a breath of fresh air You are. You seek
worshippers and then You draw us to yourself... just as
we are. Then, we are never the same. Amen

TEACHING TIP

When Jesus broke with tradition, His disciples were speechless.
Discuss: How would you have felt if you were one of them? If
you were the woman at the well?

CHAPTER TEN NOTES

READ JOHN 4:5-42

John 4:7-27
A woman of Samaria came to draw water. Jesus said to her, "Give Me a drink." For His disciples had gone away into the city to buy food. Then the woman of Samaria said to Him, "How is it that You, being a Jew, ask a drink from me, a Samaritan woman?" For Jews have no dealings with Samaritans.

Jesus answered and said to her, "If you knew the gift of God, and who it is who says to you, 'Give Me a drink,' you would have asked Him, and He would have given you living water." The woman said to Him, "Sir, You have nothing to draw with, and the well is deep. Where then do You get that living water? Are You greater than our father Jacob, who gave us the well, and drank from it himself, as well as his sons and his livestock?"

Jesus answered and said to her, "Whoever drinks of this water will thirst again, but whoever drinks of the water that I shall give him will never thirst. But the water that I shall give him will become in him a fountain of water springing up into everlasting life." The woman said to Him, "Sir, give me this water, that I may not thirst, nor come here to draw." Jesus said to her, "Go, call your husband, and come here." The woman answered and said, "I have no husband."

Jesus said to her, "You have well said, 'I have no husband,' for you have had five husbands, and the one whom you now have is not your husband; in that you spoke truly." The woman said to Him, "Sir, I perceive that You are a prophet. Our fathers worshiped on this mountain, and you Jews say that in Jerusalem is the place where one ought to worship."

Jesus said to her, "Woman, believe Me, the hour is coming when you will neither on this mountain, nor in Jerusalem, worship the Father. You worship what you do not know; we know what we worship, for salvation is of the Jews. But the hour is coming, and now is, when the true worshipers will worship the Father in spirit and truth; for the Father is seeking such to worship Him. God is Spirit, and those who worship Him must worship in spirit and truth."

The woman said to Him, "I know that Messiah is coming" (who is called Christ). "When He comes, He will tell us all things." Jesus said to her, "I who speak to you am He."

❧ 11 ☙

God's Grace for a Duet of Daughters

I t was not a vacation, though there was a boat ride to the shore where a group of greeters gathered in anticipation and expectation. Previously, Jesus had already granted great grace to others in this place; healing a royal official's child and a centurion's servant. Long-distance love healed both, because the Great Physician was not even physically present when those miracles happened. Omnipotent, all-powerful is He.

This time Jesus was so close and hope was so close that an official from the synagogue fell at the feet of the focal point of all the excitement: Jesus! He had come back to Capernaum. This man's only daughter, his little girl, was sick and dying. Time was of the essence. As the crowd pressed in upon them, Jesus and His disciples commenced to follow the father home. A miracle was about to happen, but not the one that seemed most likely to occur.

What happened next was really a miracle within a miracle. Out of the blue, right out of that crowd, a woman reached toward Jesus for help—just before the mass of people swallowed

Mark 5:22-24
And behold, one of the rulers of the synagogue came, Jairus by name. And when he saw Him, he fell at His feet and begged Him earnestly, saying, "My little daughter lies at the point of death. Come and lay Your hands on her, that she may be healed, and she will live." So Jesus went with him, and a great multitude followed Him and thronged Him.

Him from her sight. She managed to touch the hem of His cloak; He instantly knew what had happened... so did she. She was healed.

This woman for 12 years had been ritually unclean according to the Law; with an "issue of blood" (Mark 5:25). She endured more than just the monthly inconvenience common to the feminine gender; she hemorrhaged early and often. For those long, lonely years, no one was allowed to hug her or even touch her. What if she touched you? Well, that simply was not done. But she tried to reach out to touch Jesus because she had indeed tried everything else, spent all she had, and got worse. She was as desperate as the dad with the dying daughter.

Jesus looked right at the woman as she stood trembling in fear. She knew the rules. He did too: He had helped make them. But He knew something else: one day, by the shedding of His own blood, Jesus would fulfill the Law. Legalism would lose its grip, and the glorious idea of grace would be greatly strengthened. We do not know this woman's name, but we do know Jesus called her, "Daughter." He'd never done that before. With this one word, He made her part of His family.

Though this conversation did not take much time, during this short encounter word came to Jesus that the darling little daughter had died. In fact, the flute players had already arrived, along with weepers and wailers. Despair filled the air, as grief and fear sang together at the house of death.

Amidst all of that, Jesus arrived. He spoke. The crowd burst into a joyless laughter. Laughter? You might know how that feels; one moment you are crying your eyes out, and the next you are laughing hysterically with rollercoaster emotions. Grief can do that to you.

> *No one ever told me that grief felt so like fear.*
> —*C.S. Lewis[1]*

But what had Jesus just said that caused their ridicule? "The child has not died, but sleeping" (Mark 5:39). What did He do? With her mom and dad, and a few of His friends, Jesus went to the child, took her small hand, and said, "Little girl... arise!" (Mark 5:41). And so she did.

So this is our miracle within a miracle. We have a little daughter and a grown up woman called, "Daughter." One was but 12 years old, the other had suffered for those same 12 years. Both were ritually unclean, untouchable. Jesus healed both. In His inherent holiness, He remained undefiled. Law did not triumph over grace. Who could have loved them more?

As a Daughter of Eve, I am deeply touched by the tenderness of our Lord toward these two daughters. This Duet of Daughters both needed healing, at the same time. Notice that He willingly and lovingly helped both, at the right time.

Sometimes delays drive us over the moon with fear and grief. This quote from C. S. Lewis reflects our doubly deep reaction to the difficult things of life. Even though we often wish it were sooner, God in His unreasonable kindness knows exactly the right time to dazzle us with His glory.

MEDITATION

Read several times. Underline the word daughter.

Luke 8:48-49a
And He said to her, "Daughter, be of good cheer; your faith has made you well. Go in peace." While He was still speaking, someone came from the ruler of the synagogue's house, saying to him, "Your daughter is dead."

Application

One daughter is healed, the other is dead-in two short verses. What was your reaction when the first was healed? When the second died?

_____

_____

Have you ever heard someone say, "If I *only* had enough faith, I would be healed"? It is not enough to have faith in *faith*. Jesus is the object of our faith. Who was the object of the woman's faith? _____ The father's faith? _____ What is the difference between "faith in faith," and "faith in Jesus?"

_____

_____

Contemplation

Circle one and explain: How do these verses correct you? Challenge you? Calm you?

_____

_____

Personal Prayer

Lord, by grace alone through faith alone; I have received You as my Savior. I am Your child; part of Your family. Help me to keep my focus upon You: and not upon my faith. I want to worship You: not my faith. Amen.

TEACHING TIP

Discuss: How did this lesson change you? Is "faith in your faith" self-centered, or God-centered?

CHAPTER ELEVEN NOTES

READ MARK 5:21-43 (MATTHEW 9:18-26; LUKE 8:40-56)

Read Leviticus 15 for the historical background.

Leviticus 15:19-22; 26; 28-29 (Woman)
"If a woman has a discharge, and the discharge from her body is blood, she shall be set apart seven days; and whoever touches her shall be unclean until evening. Everything that she lies on during her impurity shall be unclean; also everything that she sits on shall be unclean. Whoever touches her bed shall wash his clothes and bathe in water, and be unclean until evening. If a woman has a discharge of blood for many days, other than at the time of her customary impurity, or if it runs beyond her usual time of impurity, all the days of her unclean discharge shall be as the days of her customary impurity. She shall be unclean. But if she is cleansed of her discharge, then she shall count for herself seven days, and after that she shall be clean. And on the eighth day she shall take for herself two turtledoves or two young pigeons, and bring them to the priest, to the door of the tabernacle of meeting".

Leviticus 15:1-7; 14-15 (Men)
And the Lord spoke to Moses and Aaron, saying, "Speak to the children of Israel, and say to them: 'When any man has a discharge from his body, his discharge is unclean. And this shall be his uncleanness in regard to his discharge — whether his body runs with his discharge, or his body is stopped up by his discharge, it is his uncleanness. Every bed is unclean on which he who has the discharge lies, and everything on which he sits shall be unclean. And whoever touches his bed shall wash his clothes and bathe in water, and be unclean until evening. He who sits on anything on which he who has the discharge sat shall wash his clothes and bathe in water, and be unclean until evening. And he who touches the body of him who has the discharge shall wash his clothes and bathe in water, and be unclean until evening. If he who has the discharge spits on him who is clean, then he shall wash his clothes and bathe in water, and be unclean until evening.

On the eighth day he shall take for himself two turtledoves or two young pigeons, and come before the Lord, to the door of the tabernacle of meeting, and give them to the priest. Then the priest shall offer them, the one as a sin offering and the other as a burnt offering. So the priest shall make atonement for him before the Lord because of his discharge.'"

John 4:46-51

So Jesus came again to Cana of Galilee where He had made the water wine. And there was a certain nobleman whose son was sick at Capernaum. When he heard that Jesus had come out of Judea into Galilee, he went to Him and implored Him to come down and heal his son, for he was at the point of death. Then Jesus said to him, "Unless you people see signs and wonders, you will by no means believe." The nobleman said to Him, "Sir, come down before my child dies!" Jesus said to him, "Go your way; your son lives." So the man believed the word that Jesus spoke to him, and he went his way. And as he was now going down, his servants met him and told him, saying, "Your son lives!"

Matthew 8:5-13

Now when Jesus had entered Capernaum, a centurion came to Him, pleading with Him, saying, "Lord, my servant is lying at home paralyzed, dreadfully tormented." And Jesus said to him, "I will come and heal him." The centurion answered and said, "Lord, I am not worthy that You should come under my roof. But only speak a word, and my servant will be healed. For I also am a man under authority, having soldiers under me. And I say to this one, 'Go,' and he goes; and to another, 'Come,' and he comes; and to my servant, 'Do this,' and he does it."

When Jesus heard it, He marveled, and said to those who followed, "Assuredly, I say to you, I have not found such great faith, not even in Israel! And I say to you that many will come from east and west, and sit down with Abraham, Isaac, and Jacob in the kingdom of heaven. But the sons of the kingdom will be cast out into outer darkness. There will be weeping and gnashing of teeth." Then Jesus said to the centurion, "Go your way; and as you have believed, so let it be done for you." And his servant was healed that same hour.

❧ 12 ❧

God's Grace for a not-so-Gentle Gentile

In an ancient kingdom long, long ago, and far, far away from the heartbeat of Jerusalem, a pagan princess, Jezebel, ruled with an iron glove. Strangely enough, she was married to a king of Israel. Mixed marriages can come with baggage, and she came complete with 450 pagan prophets of Baal. While evil had fairly free reign in this hugely hedonistic huddle of humanity, God was on the move. His man, Elijah, was right there in the thick of things. Cultures were about to clash with a crash when fire rained from heaven, followed later by a tiny cloud over the sea—symbolic of the very hand of God—which signaled the end of a deadly drought.

If that wasn't enough to know the Lord was God, Elijah destroyed a goodly number of ungodly prophets of the pagan princess. That made her really mad. Tired and wired, our hero Elijah ran for his life thinking he was the only hope left in that morally dry land. Do you know that God still had 7,000 people in that pagan place who had not bowed the knee to Baal? This

> **1 Kings 18:21**
> And Elijah came to all the people, and said, "How long will you falter between two opinions? If the Lord is God, follow Him; but if Baal, follow him." But the people answered him not a word.

season came to an end several years later when Jezebel was pushed from her window in the castle wall and went, quite literally, to the dogs.

This is the background behind the scrim that sets the stage for another victorious battle between good and evil and another Gentile woman. Time passed, and the God of Elijah—after sending many prophets and several angels—actually sent His perfectly sinless, only Son into the world. This fulfilled the promise in the Garden that a child of Eve would crush the head of evil.

At long last, Jesus had arrived on the scene. He had been busy. You remember the famous fish fry for the five thousand when the people tried to make Jesus the food king. Then there was the water-walking incident during the wild sea storm that wowed His boys in the boat. Finally, the Pharisees had had it with His signs and wonders, so they laid down the Law: guilty as charged! The charge? His disciples ate without washing their hands. Legalism loomed large.

Apparently, the eating of bread with unclean hands was akin to the unpardonable sin, when in fact their rejection of King Jesus and His Kingdom at that specific point in time might have been closer to the truth.

No matter, Jesus had another encounter to pursue, so He took a walkabout with His disciples right out of Israel into the very domain of darkness where Jezebel had died long ago. Enter the Syrophoenician woman, on center stage. What a piece of work she was! The disciples where aghast at her behavior, because not only had she slipped into their safe house, but she'd also managed to fall begging at the feet of Jesus. She just could not shut up. Their silence was shattered by her love for her child.

As a Daughter of Eve, I find this brief encounter between Jesus and the mother riveting. She referred to Jesus as the Son of David, the title for a Jewish King. His major mission was to the lost sheep of Israel. For this Daughter of Eve, her love and her logic were flawless,

> **Matthew 15:22b**
> "Have mercy on me, O Lord, Son of David! My daughter is severely demon possessed."

and her lineage did not matter to Jesus. Grace abounds.

When Jesus told her that it was not good to throw the children's bread to the dogs under the table, we know He was not talking about the kind of feral dogs Jezebel had encountered. Rather, these were household dogs, and she knew that even those little dogs got crumbs. That's all she wanted, just a little crumb for her daughter. And she got it...and more! Jesus said, "O woman, great is your faith! Let it be to you as you desire" (Matt. 15:28). Her daughter was healed from that very hour.

Here we see God's unreasonable kindness toward this Gentile woman and her dear daughter. The disciples pushed back on extending grace to this woman: she was downright irritating— but that did not disqualify her from the mercy of God expressed through His beloved Son, Jesus. Sometimes, when we are at our worst, God seems at His best. Who could have loved her more?

MEDITATION

Read several times out loud with emphasis on different words
each time:

Matthew 15: 25-28

Then she came and worshiped Him, saying, "Lord, help
me!" But He answered and said, "It is not good to take the
children's bread and throw it to the little dogs." And she
said, "Yes, Lord, yet even the little dogs eat the crumbs
which fall from their masters' table." Then Jesus answered
and said to her, "O woman, great is your faith! Let it be to
you as you desire." And her daughter was healed from that
very hour.

Application

Notice this mother's love and her logic. Underline what she said
that shows her love (emotion). Circle what she said that shows
her logic (mind).Explain how effective using both love and logic
are in problem-solving. Try this yourself this week.

_____

_____

Explain how Jesus gave grace to this not-so-Gentle Gentile
woman: _____

Did she earn His favor by being soft-spoken and diplomatic?

_____

How does this apply to you? _____

Contemplation

Circle one and explain: How do these verses comfort you?
Correct you? Change you? Challenge you? Calm you?

_____

_____

Personal Prayer

Lord, remind me to use my love and my logic when solving problems. Help me to be like this woman in my perseverance when I bring my problems before You.
Amen.

TEACHING TIP

Have students role-play Scripture using Matthew 15:21-28. Pay attention to the disciples' words.

CHAPTER TWELVE NOTES

READ 1 KINGS 17-19.

1 Kings 18:20-23

Ahab sent for all the children of Israel, and gathered the prophets together on Mount Carmel. And Elijah came to all the people, and said, "How long will you falter between two opinions? If the Lord is God, follow Him; but if Baal, follow him." But the people answered him not a word. Then Elijah said to the people, "I alone am left a prophet of the Lord; but Baal's prophets are four hundred and fifty men."

1 Kings 18:36-39

And it came to pass, at the time of the offering of the evening sacrifice, that Elijah the prophet came near and said, "Lord God of Abraham, Isaac, and Israel, let it be known this day that You are God in Israel and I am Your servant, and that I have done all these things at Your word. Hear me, O Lord, hear me, that this people may know that You are the Lord God, and that You have turned their hearts back to You again." Then the fire of the Lord fell and consumed the burnt sacrifice, and the wood and the stones and the dust, and it licked up the water that was in the trench. Now when all the people saw it, they fell on their faces; and they said," The Lord, He is God! The Lord, He is God!"

The Syrophoenician Woman

Matthew 15:21-28

Jesus went away from there, and withdrew into the district of Tyre and Sidon. And a Canaanite woman from that region came out and began to cry out, saying, "Have mercy on me, Lord, Son of David; my daughter is cruelly demon-possessed." But He did not answer her a word. And His disciples came and implored Him, saying, "Send her away, because she keeps shouting at us." But He answered and said, "I was sent only to the lost sheep of the house of Israel." But she came and began to bow down before Him, saying, "Lord, help me!" And He answered and said, "It is not good to take the children's bread and throw it to the dogs." But she said, "Yes, Lord; but even the dogs feed on the crumbs which fall from their masters' table." Then Jesus said to her, "O woman, your faith is great; it shall be done for you as you wish." And her daughter was healed at once.

❧ 13 ❧

God's Grace for the Accused with no Accusers

Everyone falls short of God's glory, but no one need fall short of His grace. Hope whispers in the hearts of humankind because an unreasonable kind of kindness covers the glitches that come from not being perfectly perfect. Deep within every Son of Adam and each Daughter of Eve, those hitches are like holes in our souls. It is the human condition, but each empty place can be filled with God's grace.

Some folks respond to that reality with a peculiar modus operandi. They randomly appoint themselves both judge and jury for those who fall short. This legalistic attitude comes from a biased belief that those who fail are unworthy of love and need to be punished.

A case in point involved a woman caught in adultery. In the Law, the gold standard is condensed into key decrees.

> **Deuteronomy 5:18**
> You shall not commit adultery.

From the Top Ten, number Seven comes into play in this story. When this Daughter of Eve was caught by a flock of legal eagles, it appeared to be an open-and-shut case, but it wasn't. How could that be?

The crime was committed early in the morning. The crime scene was very near the Temple: neither a typical time nor place for a tryst. A group of scribes and Pharisees were there at just the right place and just the right time to come upon "the very act." Doesn't that sound just a little creepy and slightly suspicious? They brought the gal to Jesus there at the court in the courtyard, but where was the guy?

Understanding the means, motivation and opportunity might be instructive in solving this mystery. The focus of all of this misdirection was to refute and repudiate Jesus, as the Son of God, through a premeditated plan of entrapment.

The woman was to be the means by which the trap would snap—simply collateral damage. Jesus knew it. The motivation? To test and try Truth personified. Jesus got it. Opportunity opened up when that gaggle of guys just happened to pass the place where the perps were in position. Jesus understood it.

Concerning the woman: They caught her and brought her, but what had they taught her? That mini mob was not interested in justice, or mercy, for this Daughter of Eve as they set her before Jesus. Quite the contrary, the crew was spoiling for a fight: badgering, bristling, and boiling with energy.

> The Bible is replete with commands to persevere, especially in the face of injustice.
> —*Joni Eareckson Tada*[1]

The silence of Jesus stilled their sounds. That break broke the momentum as Jesus stooped down and wrote in the dust... twice. In between those two pauses, He said, "He who is without sin among you, let him throw a stone at her first" (John 8:7). The Savior of the world saved her with His sentence. It was brilliant.

The self-same Law that permitted retribution, allowed

GOD'S GRACE FOR THE ACCUSED WITH NO ACCUSERS

for redemption. It took two, or three, witnesses to corroborate allegations of said sin. Because scribes and Pharisees were in on this plot, there were four, or possibly even more. But after Jesus stepped in, there were none. Not even one. The evidence was evidently inadmissible.

Since there was not a single sinless soul in that rabble, slowly and silently—from oldest to youngest—the men just melted away. Gone were the accusers. Only the accused remained. Jesus did not encourage license, nor did He leverage legalism. He gave liberty to this Daughter of Eve. Then the face of grace spoke these words: "Go and sin no more" (John 8:11).

This had been a preposterous predicament, planned as an unsurvivable attack on grace. Someone was going to die that day, but didn't. Though the threat level had been temporarily lowered by love, the problem was not solved. The lethality of legalism was alive and well and would live to fight another day.

As a Daughter of Eve, I marvel how Jesus slowed the action of the angry mob by writing in the dirt: twice. His words of wisdom worked. He actually gave them a timely gift: time to think. A well-placed timeout in the closing seconds of a tight game can turn the momentum and change the outcome entirely. It did that day and indeed saved the day for that Daughter of Eve with an invisible scarlet letter on her tunic. Grace abounds. Who could have loved her more?

MEDITATION

Good Biblical hermeneutics (interpretation) and good criminal investigations share common questions: Who? What? When? Why? Where? and How? Answer these questions as you read the text.

John 8:6b-9a

But Jesus stooped down and wrote on the ground with His finger, as though He did not hear. So when they continued asking Him, He raised Himself up and said to them, "He who is without sin among you, let him throw a stone at her first." And again He stooped down and wrote on the ground. Then those who heard it, being convicted by their conscience, went out one by one.

Application

Underline the words "stooped down." Circle the way Jesus framed His verdict. How much time do you think that took? If you mirrored Jesus, the next time you had a conversational confrontation, how would this help?

_____

_____

Why did Jesus give grace to the accused?

_____

When did He last give grace to you?

_____

Contemplation

Circle one and explain: How do these verses comfort you?
Correct you? Change you? Challenge you? Calm you?

_____

_____

Personal Prayer

Lord, conversational confrontation is so awkward, and usually does not end well. Thank You for showing me how to slow things down when tempers flare. Help me to do it. Amen.

TEACHING TIP

Divide people into groups of two or three Blessing Buddies, and discuss how conversational confrontation can be slowed down.

CHAPTER THIRTEEN NOTES

John 8:2-12

Now early in the morning He came again into the temple, and all the people came to Him; and He sat down and taught them. Then the scribes and Pharisees brought to Him a woman caught in adultery. And when they had set her in the midst, they said to Him, "Teacher, this woman was caught in adultery, in the very act. Now Moses, in the law, commanded us that such should be stoned. But what do You say?"

This they said, testing Him, that they might have something of which to accuse Him. But Jesus stooped down and wrote on the ground with His finger, as though He did not hear. So when they continued asking Him, He raised Himself up and said to them, "He who is without sin among you, let him throw a stone at her first."

And again He stooped down and wrote on the ground. Then those who heard it, being convicted by their conscience, went out one by one, beginning with the oldest even to the last.

And Jesus was left alone, and the woman standing in the midst. When Jesus had raised Himself up and saw no one but the woman, He said to her, "Woman, where are those accusers of yours? Has no one condemned you?" She said, "No one, Lord." And Jesus said to her, "Neither do I condemn you; go and sin no more."

Then Jesus spoke to them again, saying, "I am the light of the world. He who follows Me shall not walk in darkness, but have the light of life."

☙ 14 ❧

God's Grace in Sanctifying Sisters

She was known for her little candlelight suppers. The most noteworthy, the best and the worst, were preserved in holy writ for time and eternity. That's right—read all about it in the Bible. Our Martha almost blew it within three verses, despite—or, perhaps, because of—the presence of the guest of honor: Jesus. She had personally welcomed Him into her home for that dinner. Abounding in good works, Martha did things right, until she didn't. Mary was right there helping her, until she wasn't. What happened?

Truth be known, and it was, Martha had a lot on her mind and plate, but her bitterness was spoiling the broth. Mary loved abiding in Christ, so she slipped out. Then Martha flipped out, right in front of God and everyone, including Mary. Finally, she burst out, saying, "Lord, don't You care?... Tell her to help me," (Luke 10:40).

> "You can give without loving, but you cannot love without giving."
> —*Amy Carmichael*[1]

John 11:5-6
Now, Jesus loved Martha and her sister and Lazarus. So, when He heard that he was sick, He stayed two more days in the place where He was.

One shudders at the sound of triangulation and manipulation, particularly at a little candlelight dinner. "Martha, Martha," said Jesus. Can you almost see Him shaking His head? Yet, who could have loved her more? He specifically spoke truth into her tension. No doubt the evening ended better than it had started.

Not long after that, there was a bit of an emergency in the house at Bethany, and Jesus was asked to return. The beloved brother of those sacred sisters was sick, but, for reasons unknown to Martha and Mary, Jesus delayed His arrival. He was too late; now their brother was the late Lazarus—dead and buried.

Have you ever come across something in the Bible that seemed strange? All Scripture is inspired by God, inerrant in the original manuscripts—even the tricky parts. Why did Jesus wait? He loved this family.

He'd been good to Mary, better to Martha, but He saved the best for last, for Lazarus. Love was on the loose: grace was about to be given, and change charged the air. When He drew near to the house, Martha came out to greet Jesus, and they talked privately. She spoke confidently about her belief to the very Man she'd served so awkwardly. Then she secretly sought out and brought out her sister Mary to see Jesus. Mary wept, weepers wept, and Jesus wept. Everything was proceeding properly, until Jesus had a strange request. At the cave site—the grave site—He wanted the rock that covered the cave removed. Highly irregular it was.

Of course, Martha protested. Lazarus had been dead, after all, for four days. But he stone was moved away anyway. Jesus prayed to His Father for the benefit of those who would believe. Then He cried with a loud voice, "Lazarus, come forth!" (John 11:43). And he did: alive and well. Many believed. Wouldn't you?

Well, another little candlelight dinner was in order. As a Daughter of Eve, a silly grin lights up my life as I imagine the coming King of Israel seated serenely for supper at Martha's house—again. The scene seemed the same, but everything was different because this was now a place of grace.

Here's why: before Martha served, before Mary sat, "There they made Him a supper" (John 12:2). They did it together, the both of them. Their brother Lazarus was no longer late but alive, seated by Jesus at the table. What a celebration that must have been, but this was their Last Supper with Jesus—ever.

The very next day, Jesus entered Jerusalem riding on a young donkey as the crowd went wild, waving palm branches and shouting, "Hosanna, 'Blessed is He who comes in the name of the Lord!' The King of Israel!" (John 12:13).

These sacred sisters, set apart by the Father, were made holy and whole by Jesus. Through their suffering they learned what it meant to be saved from the power of their sins and to be comforted by God's unreasonable kindness. Grace abounds!

MEDITATION

Read several times. Underline they.

> ### John 12:1-2a
> Then six days before the Passover, Jesus came to Bethany, where Lazarus who had been dead whom He raised from the dead. There they made Him a supper.

Application

Mary and Martha: A Meal → A Miracle → A Meal
Why did Jesus give the girls another chance?

_____

Are you like sister Mary, or sister Martha? Circle one and tell why:

_____

Contemplation

Circle one and explain: How do these verses comfort you?
Correct you? Change you? Challenge you? Calm you?

_____

_____

Salvation is a Big Idea:
Justification—Saved from the penalty of sin. (Past)
Sanctification—Saved from the power of sin. (Present)
Glorification—Saved from the presence of sin. (Future)

When Martha said to Jesus, "Yes, Lord, I believe that you are the Christ, the Son of God, who is come into the world," would you say that was Justification, Sanctification, or Glorification? Why?

_____

Personal Prayer

Lord, I believe that You are the Christ, the Son of God, who is come into the world. Thank You for loving me like you loved Martha, Mary and Lazarus. Amen.

TEACHING TIP

Our God is a giver of second chances. All our sins were paid for at the cross where Jesus died less than a week after that little candlelight supper. He gave those sisters a second chance. Discuss the implications of that for sanctification.

CHAPTER FOURTEEN NOTES

Luke 10:38-11:1

Now it happened as they went that He entered a certain village; and a certain woman named Martha welcomed Him into her house. And she had a sister called Mary, who also sat at Jesus' feet and heard His word. But Martha was distracted with much serving, and she approached Him and said, "Lord, do You not care that my sister has left me to serve alone? Therefore tell her to help me." And Jesus answered and said to her, "Martha, Martha, you are worried and troubled about many things. But one thing is needed, and Mary has chosen that good part, which will not be taken away from her."

John 11:1-7

Now a certain man was sick, Lazarus of Bethany, the town of Mary and her sister Martha. It was that Mary who anointed the Lord with fragrant oil and wiped His feet with her hair, whose brother Lazarus was sick. Therefore the sisters sent to Him, saying, "Lord, behold, he whom You love is sick."

When Jesus heard that, He said, "This sickness is not unto death, but for the glory of God, that the Son of God may be glorified through it." Now Jesus loved Martha and her sister and Lazarus. So, when He heard that he was sick, He stayed two more days in the place where He was. Then after this He said to the disciples, "Let us go to Judea again."

John 11:17-18; 28; 32

So when Jesus came, He found that he had already been in the tomb four days. Now Bethany was near Jerusalem, about two miles away. And when she had said these things, she went her way and secretly called Mary her sister, saying, "The Teacher has come and is calling for you." Then, when Mary came where Jesus was, and saw Him, she fell down at His feet, saying to Him," Lord, if You had been here, my brother would not have died.

John 12:1-2; 12-13

Then, six days before the Passover, Jesus came to Bethany, where Lazarus was who had been dead, whom He had raised from the dead. There they made Him a supper; and Martha served, but Lazarus was one of those who sat at the table with Him.

The next day a great multitude that had come to the feast, when they heard that Jesus was coming to Jerusalem, took branches of palm trees and went out to meet Him, and cried out: "Hosanna!'Blessed is He who comes in the name of the Lord!' The King of Israel!"

∞ 15 ∞

God's Grace for She with Silver Coins

Growling and grumbling religious leaders were increasingly disgruntled with Jesus. While the glum spirits dug themselves deeper into their displeasure, the sinners were as excited as if Jesus had proposed a tea party followed by dancing. His was a celebratory soul, for he made statements such as, "We played the flute for you, and you did not dance."

If that wasn't enough to get their attention, He followed that with, "We sang a dirge and you did not cry." Sounds like a fairly flat affect; however, the most noticeable emotion those leaders expressed was anger.

In order to defuse the defensive, He'd take the truth and securely place it in a package called a parable. Then Jesus would pass them out, as needed, like presents. These truth-filled tales could help heal hearts bogged down with the bags and baggage of legalism. One day He brought out the package called the Lost and Found Box. It contained one sad sheep, one silver coin, and one soiled son. All were lost.

Luke 15:9-10
And when she has found it, she calls her friends and neighbors together, saying, "Rejoice with me, for I have found the piece which I lost!" Likewise, I say to you, there is joy in the presence of the angels of God over one sinner who repents.

Each was loved by the person to whom they belonged: a shepherd, a woman, a father. Even though the shepherd had more sheep; the woman more coins; the father another son, that which was lost could be found. Who could have loved them more?

A Daughter of Eve owned ten silver coins, most likely on a necklace worn as a headband on her wedding day. One treasured coin was gone, lost, leaving a hole in her soul. Remember something you lost? That loss stays in your heart, even when long gone from your life. She with Silver Coins was just like that. She became restless and relentless; she rummaged around, lit a lamp, swept the house, carefully searched, and she found it! The lost was found. The End.

But was this actually the end? No, this was just the beginning of the party. Each time the lost was found, whether the coin, the sheep, or the son, the result was the same: it was celebrated with merrymaking. Where? Actually, there were two venues for the festivities—one on earth and the other in heaven. Can you believe that? It was perfect, really, because She with Silver Coins had already cleaned her house! Then, friends and family filled it with joy. In heaven angels attended. That's right! Angels rejoiced.

The lost sheep was found: friends and neighbors gathered and rejoiced. Then Jesus said, "I say to you likewise there will be more joy in heaven over one sinner who repents than over ninety-nine just persons who need no repentance" (Luke 15:7). The lost was found.

And again, the lost son returned: friends, music and BBQ, then dancing and merrymaking, followed by the father saying, "It is right that we should make merry and be glad...your brother was lost and is found" (Luke 15:32).

Lost → Found → Party

As a daughter of Eve, I understand that it might seem unseemly to gloat, and so perhaps "to rejoice" is a better choice of words; but I can tell you that the woman, the shepherd, and the father couldn't have been happier. We cannot lose sight of what was actually found. In these Lost and Found lessons, there is a reverberation from here to eternity—when a sinner repents here there is a party in paradise.

Some would say that this is a lesson about justification, and well it might be. However, the sheep belonged to the shepherd, the coin to the woman, and the son to his father. This would indicate a lesson about sanctification. Restoration and celebration are tightly linked in the story of the Lost and the Found. Grace abounds.

MEDITATION

Read several times and underline three things this woman does.
Circle the words lost and found.

Luke 15:9-10
And when she has found it, she calls her friends and neighbors together, saying, "Rejoice with me, for I have found the piece which I lost!" Likewise, I say to you, there is joy in the presence of the angels of God, over one sinner who repents.

Application

Lost → Found → Party

Lost and found is followed by celebration. Why? _____
_____

Who celebrates? _____

Where does this merrymaking take place? _____

How do angels know? _____

Explain a time when you lost and then found something: _____
_____

How is the grace of God expressed in the life of She with Silver Coins? _____
_____

Contemplation

Circle one and explain: How do these verses comfort you?
Correct you? Change you? Challenge you? Calm you?

_____
_____

Personal Prayer

Lord, when I've lost something, help me to light a lamp, sweep the house, and search carefully. When I find what was lost, remind me to call friends and neighbors to rejoice together. Amen

TEACHING TIP

Have your students close their eyes and picture the Lord as shepherd as you read Psalm 23. "The Lord is my shepherd..."

CHAPTER FIFTEEN NOTES

Matthew 11:17b-19
"'We played the flute for you, and you did not dance; we mourned to you, and you did not lament. For John came neither eating nor drinking, and they say, 'He has a demon.' The Son of Man came eating and drinking, and they say, 'Look, a glutton and a winebibber, a friend of tax collectors and sinners!' But wisdom is justified by her children."

Luke 15:4-8
"What man of you, having a hundred sheep, if he loses one of them, does not leave the ninety-nine in the wilderness, and go after the one which is lost until he finds it? And when he has found it, he lays it on his shoulders, rejoicing. And when he comes home, he calls together his friends and neighbors, saying to them, 'Rejoice with me, for I have found my sheep which was lost!' I say to you that likewise there will be more joy in heaven over one sinner who repents than over ninety-nine just persons who need no repentance."

Luke 15:8-11
"Or what woman, having ten silver coins, if she loses one coin, does not light a lamp, sweep the house, and search carefully until she finds it? And when she has found it, she calls her friends and neighbors together, saying, 'Rejoice with me, for I have found the piece which I lost!' Likewise, I say to you, there is joy in the presence of the angels of God over one sinner who repents."

Luke 15:22-24
"But the father said to his servants, 'Bring out the best robe and put it on him, and put a ring on his hand and sandals on his feet. And bring the fatted calf here and kill it, and let us eat and be merry; for this my son was dead and is alive again; he was lost and is found.' And they began to be merry."

Psalm 23
The Lord is my shepherd; I shall not want. He makes me to lie down in green pastures; He leads me beside the still waters. He restores my soul; He leads me in the paths of righteousness for His name's sake. Yea, though I walk through the valley of the shadow of death, I will fear no evil; For You are with me; Your rod and Your staff, they comfort me. You prepare a table before me in the presence of my enemies; You anoint my head with oil; my cup runs over. Surely goodness and mercy shall follow all the days of my life; and I will dwell in the house of the Lord, forever.

God's Grace for Lovers, Mothers, and Others

Everything that could go wrong did: right on time. Professional pessimism reached a record-breaking high. Orthodox worriers were everywhere, but nowhere near the cross. John the Beloved Disciple was there. And Jesus was there: on that cross. Right across from the cross were his mother and others. Daughters of Eve were everywhere.

This was the lowest of low points because Jesus was dying for the worst of the worst and quite surprisingly, for the best of the best. All are perfectly imperfect. All by their very human nature have fallen short of the glory of God. Yet all are loved lavishly by the lover of their souls. From before the beginning, a plan began to make things right. When Adam and Eve thought they had fallen from grace, they actually fell right into the embrace of the grace of God.

Eve was promised two things before leaving the Garden: though the serpent who seduced her would bruise a blessed baby of a Daughter of Eve, that same wounded offspring would inflict a cranial concussion upon the shining evil one that would cause death to die. Grace abounds.

All of those prayers and promises woven by the hands of God through the tangles of time were about to be realized, but what was right seemed to have gone terribly wrong. The child of a Daughter of Eve was the one who was dying.

War walked down the corridors of time. Soldiers dying in battle are sometimes heard to call out for their mothers. On the cross, Jesus, the wounded warrior, called out to his mother and gave her to His disciple, the beloved John, for safekeeping. Then from his cross, He shouted forth a battle cry of victory that sounded from there to eternity: "It is finished!" (John 19:30).

That which was the lowest of low became the highest of high when Jesus gave His life to ransom those He loved.

The mother, and the others, had often seen in Jesus the face of grace, and were in that place of grace when they felt the earth shake and quake as Life died. Strange things started to happen. Nearby in the Temple, the veil that had separated the Glory of the Lord from the people of the Lord suddenly sheared in two: from top to bottom. This was earth-shattering in its impact because the invisible presence of God was known to have had been present in the Holy of Holies behind that veil. But now, well, nothing was there. Where was the Glory of the Lord? Wouldn't you want to know?

A long time ago, the Glory of the Lord was in the cloud on Mt. Sinai when Moses received the Law given to the people of promise after they escaped from Egypt. The Glory of the Lord was in the Tabernacle in the wilderness and led the people of the Lord to the land of promise. After David's son, Solomon, built the Temple in Jerusalem, the Glory of the Lord filled the Temple of the Lord. Time passed, then the elders of the Lord turned their backs on the Lord. This had not happened

> *When a willing victim who had committed no treachery was killed in a traitor's stead, the Table would crack and Death would start working backwards.*
>
> **— C.S. Lewis**[1]

overnight. It took years and years. The people were drawn to other gods, even though the very presence of their God was right there in the Holy of Holies, that Holy Place.

Then it happened: The Glory of the Lord was on the move—it filled the inner court of the Temple, paused at the threshold, and went out the door of the East Gate. Then Glory of the Lord left the house.

Remember, when Jesus was born the Glory of the Lord shown all about: it filled the sky above the manger. After Jesus, the Lord of Glory, died,there was great mourning by the Daughters of Eve;by Lovers, Mothers and Others, but there were things to be done. In the darkness of dawn that first Easter morn, a group of them went to the garden tomb where Jesus was buried. The spices they'd brought were completely unnecessary. His body was gone! How could they know that? Because the tomb was open. What about the stone, the seal and the Roman guards? Sitting sedately on that stone was an angel, right in front of the shaking and quaking soldiers, whom the angel ignored. But to the women he said, "Do not be afraid...He is risen!" (Matt. 28:5). Then Daughters of Eve—amazed, astonished and still a little afraid—left to tell the disciples. These women were eyewitnesses to the events called the Gospel: Jesus died for our sins, He was buried, and He rose again. Life lived!

As a Daughter of Eve, I can neither imagine the loss of the mother and the others, nor completely understand their joy when they saw Jesus again. But what I do know is that both promises in that first Garden were fulfilled: Jesus was bruised unto death for our sins, and He rose bodily from the grave in victory over the evil one. He conquered death. His grace is free, because

> *If you've been up all night and cried till you have no more tears left in you - you will know that there comes in the end a sort of quietness. You feel as if nothing was ever going tohappen again.*
> — *C.S. Lewis*[2]

He willingly bore the cost. Jesus loves us. This we know. The stone Table was broken, death started working backward, giving life that will last forever by grace alone, through faith alone, in Christ alone. What about the Glory of the Lord?

Scripture says it best in 1 Corinthians 6:19-20: "Do you not know that your body is the temple of the Holy Spirit who is in you, whom you have from God, and you are not your own? For you were bought at a price; therefore glorify God in your body and in your spirit, which are God's." Who could have loved us more? This is God's amazing grace, and now Lovers, Mothers, and Others, can be the face of grace in their world.

MEDITATION

Read several times. Underline the word glory. Circle the phrase vessels of mercy.

Romans 9:23-25

And that He might make known the riches of His glory on the vessels of mercy, which He had prepared beforehand for glory, even us whom He called, not of the Jews only, but also of the Gentile. As He says also in Hosea:"I will call them My people, who were not My people, and her beloved, who was not beloved."

Application

Who are the *vessels of mercy* mentioned in these verses? _____
_____

What two people groups are noted? _____
How is God's grace shown to Lovers, Mothers and Others? _____
_____

What does it mean to you to be *beloved* of God? _____

Contemplation

Circle one and explain: How do these verses comfort you?
Challenge you? Calm you? Change you?

_____

_____

Personal Prayer

Lord, thank You for creating me in Your image. Thank You for blessing me. Grant me the courage to cooperate with the good You have planned for me. Show Your grace to me today. Amen

TEACHING TIP

From memory, list the movement of the manifestation of the Glory of the Lord from Moses to us. Use the Scripture on the next page if you need prompts.

CHAPTER SIXTEEN NOTES

As we trace the presence of the Glory of the Lord from Moses on Mt. Sinai, to the Tabernacle in the wilderness, in the Holy of Holies in the Temple, and finally out the door of the east gate in the Temple, we are amazed and astounded to discover when Jesus was born the Glory of the Lord returned.

Glory of the Lord in the Wilderness (Exodus 16:6-7a,10)
Then Moses and Aaron said to all the children of Israel, "At evening you shall know that the Lord has brought you out of the land of Egypt. And in the morning you shall see the glory of the Lord. Now it came to pass, as Aaron spoke to the whole congregation of the children of Israel, that they looked toward the wilderness, and behold, the glory of the Lord appeared in the cloud.

Glory of the Lord on Mt. Sinai (Exodus24:16)
Now the glory of the Lord rested on Mount Sinai, and the cloud covered it six days. And on the seventh day He called to Moses out of the midst of the cloud.

Glory of the Lord in the Tabernacle (Exodus 40:34)
Then the cloud covered the tabernacle of meeting, and the glory of the Lord filled the tabernacle.

Glory of the Lord in the Holy Place in the Temple (1 Kings 8:10-11)
And it came to pass, when the priests came out of the holy place, that the cloud filled the house of the Lord, so that the priests could not continue ministering because of the cloud; for the glory of the Lord filled the house of the Lord.

Glory of the Lord Read Ezekiel 8:15-11:22 for the context of the following content:

Glory of the Lord Leaves the Cherub (Ezekiel 9:3 and 10:4)
Now the glory of the God of Israel had gone up from the cherub, where it had been, to the threshold of the temple. Then the glory of the Lord went up from the cherub, and paused over the threshold of the temple; and the house was filled with the cloud, and the court was full of the brightness of the Lord's glory.

Glory of the Lord Leaves the Threshold (Ezekiel 10:18-19 and 11:23)
Then the glory of the Lord departed from the threshold of the temple and stood over the cherubim. And the cherubim lifted their wings and mounted up from the earth in my sight. When they went out, the wheels were beside them; and they stood at the

door of the east gate of the Lord's house, and the glory of the God of Israel was above them. And the glory of the Lord went up from the midst of the city and stood on the mountain, which is on the east side of the city.

Glory of the Lord Returns at the Birth of Jesus (Luke 2:8-12)
Now there were in the same country shepherds living out in the fields, keeping watch over their flock by night. And behold, an angel of the Lord stood before them, and the glory of the Lord shone around them, and they were greatly afraid. Then the angel said to them,"Do not be afraid, for behold, I bring you good tidings of great joy which will be to all people. For there is born to you this day in the city of David a Savior, who is Christ the Lord. And this will be the sign to you: You will find a Babe wrapped in swaddling cloths, lying in a manger."

The Veil Torn (Matthew 27:51-56)
Then, behold, the veil of the temple was torn in two from top to bottom; and the earth quaked, and the rocks were split, and the graves were opened; and many bodies of the saints who had fallen asleep were raised; and coming out of the graves after His resurrection, they went into the holy city and appeared to many. So when the centurion and those with him, who were guarding Jesus, saw the earthquake and the things that had happened, they feared greatly, saying, "Truly this was the Son of God!" And many women who followed Jesus from Galilee, ministering to Him, were there looking on from afar, among whom were Mary Magdalene, Mary the mother of James and Joses, and the mother of Zebedee's sons.

හ 17 ශ

God's Grace for the Beloved Bride

T he rest of the story is the best of the story, because history reminds us of the transcendent truth of God's faithfulness. As you have seen through the lives of Daughters of Eve, God's love is expressed through His astonishing grace which is unmerited, unearned, undeniable and unending, yet believably believable. Who could have loved us more?

Just at the right time, what was planned before time was braided into the tangles of time, by God's grace and for His glory. The history of God's everlasting love also is observed by the geography of His unending faithfulness: Israel exists. Against overwhelming odds, the land of promise and the people of promise were once again united...in 1948. It is right there on the map.

This is the land of the Warrior Woman, the Widow with Wisdom, and the Girl Next Door, as well as the

> **Jeremiah 31:3**
> The Lord has appeared of old to me, saying: "Yes, I have loved you with an everlasting love; Therefore with loving kindness I have drawn you."

Momma by the Manger, the Duet of Daughters, Mothers, Lovers, and Others: Daughters of Eve who are all resplendent recipients of God's unreasonable kindness, His amazing grace.

Remember the not Gentle Gentile? The disciples pushed back on extending grace to this woman: she was categorically and completely irritating, like fingernails screeching down a broken old blackboard. But that did not disqualify her from the mighty mercy of God expressed through the beloved Son of God, because God so loved the world. He is all in; for all of us.

By nature and nurture all are intrinsically self-centered and self-serving, all have fallen short of the glory of God. It would take an *Act of God* to override this natural bent toward self, sin, and separation. God knew He could do anything, so He did everything.

Not only did God offer redemption through the Messiah, but He also offered reconciliation. The Acts of God in bringing Jews and Gentiles to Him—and together—are recorded interestingly enough in a book of the Bible called Acts. Thus the church, the Bride of Christ, was born. The love between Jesus and His church is explained in terms of the way a husband can love his beloved bride.

Ephesians 5:25-27
Husbands, love your wives, just as Christ also loved the church and gave Himself for her, that He might sanctify and cleanse her with the washing of water by the word, that He might present her to Himself a glorious church, not having spot or wrinkle or any such thing, but that she should be holy and without blemish.

How on earth is this possible? Legalism requires love—though rarely experiences it—license often interprets lust as love-and misses it, but liberty encourages love-and gives it. When a believer is rescued from legalism, or license, there is a freedom to love lavishly like Jesus loved, with a holy, happy, healthy kind of unreasonable kindness that expresses itself by doing the good things God has for us to do.

Grace abounds for the Beloved Bride as she experiences, then expresses, God's love, joy, peace, patience, kindness, goodness, faithfulness, gentleness, and self-control. It is not only possible

> *You have not chosen one another, but I have chosen you for one another.*
> —*C.S. Lewis*[1]

but quite probable, normal but not natural—and that is the glitch. The life that was received by grace alone, through faith alone, in Christ alone, is lived the very same way: by grace alone, through faith alone, in Christ alone.

Not only has Jesus saved us, but He also now sanctifies us and secures us. As a Daughter of Eve, one of my deepest needs is security. Jesus said, "And I give them eternal life, and they shall never perish; neither shall anyone snatch them out of My hand. My Father, who has given them to Me, is greater than all; and no one is able to snatch them out of My Father's hand. I and My Father are one" (John 10:28-30). This secures the believer to lavishly enjoy God's love in this life...and in the life to come, to be rewarded liberally for living in righteous deeds, by God's grace and for His glory.

MEDITATION

Notice that we are saved by grace to live by grace. Put one line under the phrase, "not of works." Put two lines under the phrase, "created in Christ Jesus for good works."

Ephesians 2:8-10
For by grace you have been saved through faith, and that not of yourselves; it is the gift of God, not of works, lest anyone should boast, for we are His workmanship, created in Christ Jesus for good works, which God prepared beforehand that we should walk in them.

Now, put two lines under "the righteous acts of the saints," in the following text:

Revelation 19:6-9
And I heard, as it were, the voice of a great multitude, as the sound of many waters and as the sound of mighty thunderings, saying, "Alleluia! For the Lord God Omnipotent reigns! Let us be glad and rejoice and give Him glory, for the marriage of the Lamb has come, and His wife has made herself ready." And to her it was granted to be arrayed in fine linen, clean and bright, for the fine linen is the righteous acts of the saints. Then he said to me, "Write: 'Blessed are those who are called to the marriage supper of the Lamb!'"

Application

Observe that the way we live life on earth *now*. . .by God's grace and for His glory. . .has a ripple effect in *eternity*. . .by God's grace and for His glory. . .*forever.*

_____

_____

Contemplation

Circle one and explain: How do these verses comfort you? Correct you? Change you? Challenge you? Calm you?

_____

_____

Personal Prayer

Lord, thank you for saving me and securing me. Help me to live in the good works, the righteous acts, You have prepared for me, by Your grace for Your glory. Amen.

TEACHING TIP

Because of God's lavish love for us, we are saved by grace alone through faith alone in Christ alone. Because of His unreasonable kindness to us, we can live by grace alone, through faith alone in Christ alone. It is all by His grace. It is all for His glory.

CHAPTER SEVENTEEN NOTES
READ JOHN 10 AND 14

John 10:28-30
"And I give them eternal life, and they shall never perish; neither shall anyone snatch them out of My hand. My Father, who has given them to Me, is greater than all; and no one is able to snatch them out of My Father's hand. I and My Father are one."

John 14:15-18
"And I will pray the Father, and He will give you another Helper, that He may abide with you forever—the Spirit of truth, whom the world cannot receive, because it neither sees Him nor knows Him; but you know Him, for He dwells with you and will be in you. I will not leave you orphans; I will come to you."

John 14:1-3
"Let not your heart be troubled; you believe in God, believe also in Me. In My Father's house are many mansions; if it were not so, I would have told you. I go to prepare a place for you. And if I go and prepare a place for you, I will come again and receive you to Myself; that where I am, there you may be also."

Galatians 5:22-26
But the fruit of the Spirit is love, joy, peace, long suffering, kindness, goodness, faithfulness, gentleness, self-control. Against such there is no law. And those who are Christ's have crucified the flesh with its passions and desires. If we live in the Spirit, let us also walk in the Spirit. Let us not become conceited, provoking one another, envying one another.

1 Corinthians13:1-13
Though I speak with the tongues of men and of angels, but have not love, I have become sounding brass or a clanging cymbal. And though I have the gift of prophecy, and understand all mysteries and all knowledge, and though I have all faith, so that I could remove mountains, but have not love, I am nothing. And though I bestow all my goods to feed the poor, and though I give my body to be burned, but have not love, it profits me nothing.

Love suffers long and is kind; love does not envy; love does not parade itself, is not puffed up; does not behave rudely, does not seek its own, is not provoked, thinks no evil; does not rejoice in iniquity, but rejoices in the truth; bears all things, believes all things, hopes all things, endures all things. Love never fails. But whether there are prophecies, they will fail; whether there are tongues, they will cease; whether there is knowledge, it will vanish away. For we know in part and we prophesy in part .But when that which is perfect has come, then that which is in part will be done away.

When I was a child, I spoke as a child, I understood as a child, I thought as a child; but when I became a man, I put away childish things. For now we see in a mirror, dimly, but then face to face. Now I know in part, but then I shall know just as I also am known. And now abide faith, hope, love, these three; but the greatest of these is love.

NOTES

Chapter 1

1. Elisabeth Elliot Gren, quoted in AZ Quotes, accessed August 4, 2015, http://www.azquotes.com/quote/823946.

Chapter 2

1. Joni Eareckson Tada, quoted in BrainyQuote, accessed July 15, 2015, http://www.brainyquote.com/quotes/quotes/j/jonieareck526384.html.

Chapter 3

1. Beth Moore, *Believing God Day by Day: Growing Your Faith All Year Long* (Nashville: Broadman & Holman, 2004), 28.

Chapter 4

1. Priscilla Shirer, *Discerning the Voice of God: How to Recognize When God Speaks* (Nashville: Lifeway Christian Resources, 2012), 133.

Chapter 5

1. C.S. Lewis, quoted in BrainyQuote, accessed August 4, 2015, http://www.brainyquote.com/quotes/quotes/c/cslewis100842.html.

Chapter 6

1. Beth Moore, *A Heart Like His: Intimate Reflections on the Life of David* (Nashville: Broadman & Holman, 2012), 10.

Chapter 7

1. Mother Teresa, quoted in Goodreads, accessed July 21, 2015, http://www.goodreads.com/ quotes/139679-love-is-not-patronizing-and-charity-isn-t-about-pity-it.

Chapter 8
1. Anne Graham Lotz, quoted in Tony Carnes, "Anne Graham Lotz: 'Nothing God Won't Forgive,'"Christianity Today, accessed July 29, 2015, http://www.christianitytoday.com/gleanings/2009/september/anne-graham-lotz-nothing-god-wont-forgive.html.

Chapter 9
1. Gigi Graham Tchividjian, quoted in The Ranch, accessed July 21, 2015, http://theranch.org/2015/01/21/gigi-graham-tchividjian-make-the-least-of-all-that-goes/.

Chapter 11
1. C.S. Lewis, *A Grief Observed* (New York: HarperCollins, 1989), accessed July 29, 2015, https://books.google.com/books?id=uK-M_IgqvuYC&printsec=frontcover&dq=a+grief+observed&hl=en&sa=X&ved=0CCcQ6AEwAGoVChMIvovu6YCBxwIVSc6ACh3XSAeu#v=onepage&q=a%20grief%20observed&f=false.

Chapter 13
1. Joni Eareckson Tada, quoted in Eryn Sun, "Joni Eareckson Tada on Wilberforce Award, 'Better Off Dead Than Disabled' Mentality," The Christian Post, accessed July 21, 2015, http://www.christianpost.com/news/joni-eareckson-tada-on-wilberforce-award-better-off-dead-than-disabled-mentality-71536/#jXZpubd4zSQoPxXt.99.

Chapter 14
1. Amy Carmichael, quoted in History Makers: The Fuel of Missions Flame, accessed July 21, 2015, http://www.historymakers.info/inspirational-christians/amy-carmichael.html.

Chapter 16

1. C. S. Lewis, *The Lion, the Witch and the Wardrobe* (New York: HarperCollins, 2000), 163.
2. Ibid., 158.

Chapter 17

1. Lewis, *The Four Loves* (Boston: Houghton Mifflin Harcourt, 1971), 89, accessed July 29, 2015, https://books.google.com/books?id=0qoftMnQ1rAC&printsec=frontcover&dq=The+Four+Loves&hl=en&sa=X&ved=0CCkQuwUwAGoVChMIktroh5z-xgIVCzk-Ch1dOAlm#v=onepage&q=%22You%20have%20not%20chosen%20one%20another%2C%20but%20I%20have%20chosen%20you%20for%20one%20another.%22&f=false.

CPSIA information can be obtained at www.ICGtesting.com
Printed in the USA
LVOW04s0305201015

458908LV00019B/152/P